Computing Perspectives

MAURICE V. WILKES

Morgan Kaufmann Publishers, Inc.
San Francisco, California

Executive Editor Bruce M. Spatz
Production Manager Yonie Overton
Assistant Editor Douglas Sery
Assistant Production Editor Julie Pabst
Composition/Text and Cover Design Jim Love/Publishers Design Studio
Copyeditor Steven Hiatt
Proofreader Ken DellaPenta
Indexer Elinor Lindheimer
Printer BookCrafters

Morgan Kaufmann Publishers, Inc.
Editorial and Sales Office
340 Pine Street, Sixth Floor
San Francisco, CA 94104-3205
USA
Telephone 415/392-2665
Facsimile 415/982-2665
Internet mkp@mkp.com

Printed in the United States of America

99 98 97 96 95 5 4 3 2 1

Library of Congress Cataloging-in-Publication Data is available for this book.
ISBN 1-55860-317-4

Contents

Contents

Preface

Computing is still a relatively new field and its technology continues to develop at a rate that is truly astonishing. At one time, when the subject was emerging from its crude beginnings, it could be said that anything that happened before yesterday was largely irrelevant. One cannot say that today. I have been engaged in the field as an observer and a participant for a good many years and it is my firm belief that the increasingly complex technology of the present time can only be fully understood—and its potential for further development evaluated—if it is seen against the background of earlier happenings.

I have called the essays in this book "perspectives" because the events and technologies discussed require some interpretation and we all tend to see things in our own way. I hope that the material that I present, along with the arguments that I advance, will help readers to sharpen their existing personal perspectives on the current state of computer science and engineering.

In putting the essays together, I have had in mind particularly students, and their teachers, together with computer professionals generally. However, much of the material is of a general kind and I hope that it will prove of value to anyone who has an interest in science and its development, and who wishes to understand where computers are going and why they are important in today's world.

The early part of the book contains a sketch of the way the computer field has developed, with an emphasis on the history of ideas rather than on the history of technology. Later, I discourse, with a similar emphasis, on a diverse range of topics from CMOS and chip design to communications and computer security. There is a communality between these topics that is not well brought out when they are treated as individual specialities and I hope that my book will help readers to see them as part of the greater whole.

Overview of the Book

It was natural for me to start the book with a piece about Charles Babbage, since I have had a long-standing interest in his work. Most easily available accounts of Babbage were written before his notebooks—"scribbling books," as he called them—were seriously examined and tend to stress his eccentricities and his failure to produce a working machine. Now it is possible to appreciate the highly original work he did on the design of computing mechanisms.

In the essays that follow, I mention the Harvard Mark I, the ENIAC, and other early machines and explain their historical importance. However, since I am concerned with ideas rather than with technology, I do not expect readers to rush to a library to look up details of all the primitive machines that I mention. However, for the benefit of those who are interested, I do provide a number of historical references in the section headed "General References" at the end of the book.

The last ten years have seen steady progress in CMOS and we have come to expect a quadrupling of chip capacity and a doubling of speed every two years. This progress, accentuated by the intellectual advances associated with the RISC movement, have led to very elegant and streamlined designs for processors. The development of windowing systems, such as X-windows and Microsoft Windows, must also be counted a success story, although the terms elegant and streamlined can hardly be applied to the underlying operating systems, which are the subject of Essay 11. The process of steady improvisation and adaptation has led to conceptual confusion and it is hard to see the wood for the trees. I believe that I am not the only long-term observer of operating system progress who feels that the subject has run away from him.

A number of the later essays deal with the relationship between telecommunications and computers. Although it has long been clear that the two industries were destined to come closer together, telecommunications engineers and computer engineers have not always found it easy to understand each other's point of view. One sign that this is now changing is the appeal that ATM (asynchronous transfer mode) has for many engineers in both industries.

Many people foresaw the great growth of computer communications, but few properly appreciated the extent to which fiber optics would make wide bandwidths available at very low cost. The working out of the consequences of this startling development has hardly begun. Let us hope that fiber optics will not constitute a destabilizing force in the telecommunications industry to the extent that CMOS has done in the computer industry.

Solitons have a romantic history and many people are curious about them. The story started in 1834, when Scott Russell saw a heap of water moving along a canal and pursued it on horseback. He recognized the phenomenon as being governed by a nonlinear differential equation. The solution of this equation in 1967 by analytical means was a remarkable achievement. It was soon found that the same method could be used to solve the corresponding equation for optical solitons in fibers. The bibliography will enable interested readers to study the subject in more detail than I provide in my essay.

The last two essays deal with computer security considered from a business point of view. My belief is that the coming into use of client-server systems, in business as elsewhere, has greatly facilitated the establishment of secure systems.

It is inevitable that, given the scope of this book, some of the views that I express should be controversial. I would like to feel that, whatever they are, they will lead to healthy argument. I would be glad to receive comments from readers.

Acknowledgements

This book is based on material drawn from a variety of sources, together with material written specially for it. The older material has been drastically rewritten and rearranged, both to reduce overlapping and to bring it up to date. In the period between April 1990 and July 1993, I wrote a series of columns for the *Communications of the ACM*. These, suitably updated, form a major part of the present book. In 1993, I delivered two invited lectures, one in May to the Federated Research Computing Conference held in San Diego, California and one in December to the 14th ACM Symposium on Operating System Principles held in Ashville, North Carolina. I have made full use of this material, although events are moving so fast that, right up to the moment of going to press, I have felt impelled to make updates and add new material. I have also drawn on the Clifford Paterson Lecture, 1990, which I delivered in November of that year to the Royal Society in London. I would like to thank the ACM and the Royal Society for allowing me to incorporate in this book material of which they hold the copyright.

The essay on artificial intelligence had its origin in an address that Donald Mickie invited me to give in 1990 to an AI dining club in Glasgow, Scotland. I am indebted to him for his sympathetic comments and for his continued inputs. Since the essay appeared as a column in *CACM*, I have added some annotations and some references to a relevant paper by John McCarthy.

I owe a special debt to the many colleagues with whom I have discussed computer topics over the years. I would like to thank especially those who provided me with information, or helped me to sort out my ideas, when I was working on the material that eventually went to make up this book. I am particularly indebted to the following for guidance on specific issues: D.D. Clark, P.J. Denning, J. Donahue, J. Dongarra, J. Dyon, D.A. Gaubatz, J.L. Hennessy, A. Hopper, N. Jouppi, N.M. Maclaren, D. May, M.D. McIlroy, R.M. Needham, B. Stroustrup, C.P. Thacker, N. Wirth, and N.E. Wiseman.

It is a pleasure to thank Jan Lee for the invaluable assistance he gave me in putting together the references. It is also a pleasure to thank Andy Hopper, Director of Corporate Research for Olivetti and Director of the Olivetti Research Laboratory in Cambridge, England, for making it possible for me to write this book, and to thank Bruce Spatz of Morgan Kaufmann Publishers for the unfailing support he gave me when I was hammering it into shape.

Maurice V. Wilkes

Cambridge, England

PART ONE

History

ESSAY ONE

Charles Babbage—The Great Uncle of Computing

On 26 December 1791, just over 200 years ago, Charles Babbage was born, son to a rising banker, at his father's home not far from a famous inn, the Elephant and Castle, in London. Some three months earlier Michael Faraday had been born, son of a blacksmith, a few hundred yards away.

Faraday's researches on electromagnetism and other subjects singled him out in his own lifetime as one of the most original and productive experimental physicists of the nineteenth century. Charles Babbage was not in the same class, and his present fame as an ancestral figure in the history of computers is a result of the spectacular success of the digital computer in our own day. However, this fame is well deserved; although his practical achievements were limited, he was the first to see clearly what might be achieved by the mechanization of computational processes.

Babbage had no immediate successor, and it was not until the first digital computers were working in the middle of the present century that people began to take a renewed interest in his ideas. The fact that there is no direct line of development from Babbage to the present day

I *Charles Babbage, late in life. This woodcut appeared in the* Illustrated London News *on 3 November 1871, shortly after Babbage's death.*
(Courtesy of Charles Babbage Institute, University of Minnesota.)

has led Doran Swade, Curator of the Computing and Control Collections at the Science Museum in London, to suggest that Babbage is not to be regarded as the father or grandfather of computing—he is more of a great uncle.

The Difference Engine

Babbage's first idea was not, in fact, a very good one, although he would never admit it. It was for a machine he called his *Difference Engine* and which he claimed would enable mathematical tables to be computed mechanically—by steam, as he once put it. However, all that a difference engine can actually do is to compute and tabulate polynomials. It is true that any mathematical function can be represented piecewise by a series of polynomials, but Babbage would have had to do a lot of paper and pencil computation in order to calculate the coefficients to be set on the engine. It was therefore more than a little misleading to say that a difference engine could compute mathematical tables. Babbage's defense would have been that he was concerned not so much with reducing human labor as with eliminating human mistakes, and that the Difference Engine would mechanize just those parts of the work in which human errors were particularly likely to occur.

Babbage presented his proposals to the British government in 1823 and they agreed to finance the construction of the Difference Engine. We are now so used to the idea of governments providing financial support to scientists and inventors that it is easy to overlook the fact that such a grant was then almost unprecedented. All went well until 1832 when Babbage had a disagreement with his engineer and work stopped. Things drifted on until 1842 when the government of the day had to decide whether to continue with the project or to terminate it. By then £17,000 (equivalent at the time to $85,000) had been expended and it appeared likely that as much again would be required.

The government cannot be accused of taking the matter lightly. On the contrary; they made wide consultations both directly and through the Royal Society. An important part was played by G.B. Airy, Astronomer Royal and head of the Royal Observatory at Greenwich. This was the only truly scientific establishment that the British government of those years possessed, and Airy was quite used to acting as scientific adviser to the government in a variety of roles that had little to do with astronomy.

Airy was hard working and his judgement was sound. He may be regarded as the prototype of the senior government scientist of today. After going into the matter very thoroughly and making his own enquiries, Airy advised the government against sinking further money in the Difference Engine and the government took his advice.

Babbage was infuriated by the decision, and from that time on had a pronounced chip on his shoulder against the British government and all its works. This comes out in his writings, particularly in his autobiography published towards the end of his life. Many modern writers have taken what Babbage said at its face value and charged the British government of the day with criminal shortsightedness.

One frequently made charge can confidently be disposed of. In declining to put more money into Babbage's Difference Engine the government did not delay the development of the digital computer. The Difference Engine was a special-purpose device for aiding in the computation of mathematical tables, and was in no sense the ancestor of the modern digital computer.

Personally, I do not see how the decision that the government eventually took can be faulted. It was not true that the Difference Engine was going to revolutionize the making of mathematical tables. This was shown clearly enough some ten years later when Georg and Edvard Scheutz, two Swedish engineers (father and son), built a successful difference engine. Their information was obtained from an article describing Babbage's ideas that had been published in a technical magazine some years earlier. The Scheutz engine did what it was supposed to and was purchased for the Dudley Observatory in Albany, New York. A copy was made for the Registrar General's office in London, an office which corresponds to the U.S. Bureau of the Census.

The Registrar General's office published a life table printed in part from plates prepared from stereo molds produced by the engine. However, in spite of the personal interest of William Farr, who was responsible for the life table, the engine soon dropped out of use. The engine at the Dudley Observatory was used to compute a refraction table, but it too dropped out of use.

The exact reasons are not recorded in either case. No doubt one was that the engines were not very reliable. They were, I suspect, apt to make occasional random mistakes. Since Babbage

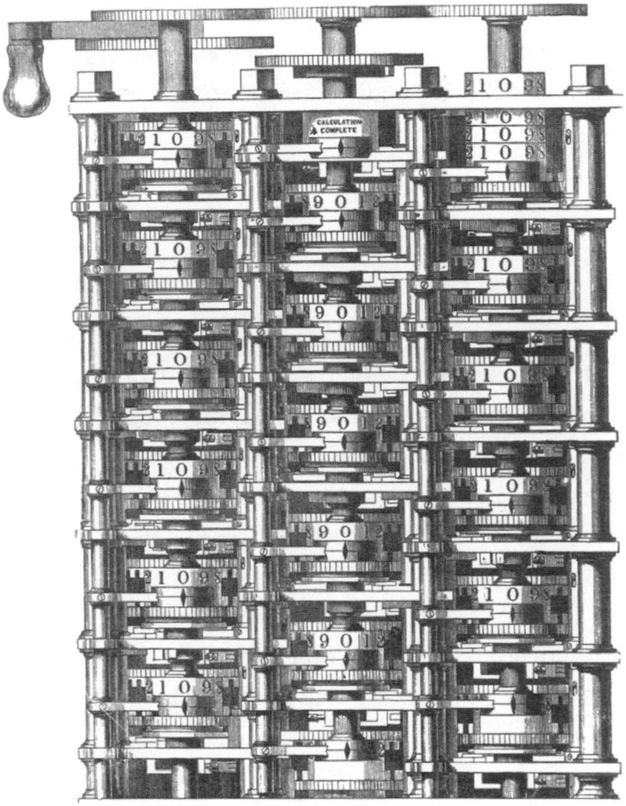

B. H. Babbage, del.

Impression from a woodcut of a small portion of Mr. Babbage's Difference Engine No. 1, the property of Government, at present deposited in the Museum at South Kensington.

It was commenced 1823.
This portion put together 1833.
The construction abandoned 1842.
This plate was printed June, 1853.
This portion was in the Exhibition 1862.

2 *This woodcut formed the frontispiece to Babbage's book,* Passages from the Life of a Philosopher, *published in 1864, and is reproduced here with the original caption. It is based on a drawing by Babbage's eldest son, Herschel, who was, among many other things, an accomplished artist. The portion of the engine illustrated is now preserved in the Science Museum, London.*

(Courtesy of Charles Babbage Institute, University of Minnesota.)

had stressed so strongly the supposed inability of machines to make mistakes this was a serious matter. However, it cannot be the whole story. If the engines were imperfect, steps could have been taken to improve them. The truth must be that the Scheutz engines were not seen as heralding a major revolution in the making of tables.

The Analytical Engine

If Babbage had stopped at the Difference Engine little more would have been heard of him. But he went on to the *Analytical Engine* which, if it had been built, would have been a true general-purpose computer—not a stored program computer in the modern sense, but more like the Harvard Mark I. Here Babbage showed insights and vision verging on genius.

A good deal was published in Babbage's lifetime about this vision—about what the Analytical Engine would do and what it might be used for. Information about the mechanical contrivances that Babbage conceived for its implementation remained hidden in his manuscript notebooks. When I examined these in detail in preparation for a lecture to be delivered on the centennial of his death in 1871, I was taken aback by the richness of what I found. He discusses the design of adding mechanisms with fast carry propagation, scales of notation, control systems, and much else besides. If Babbage had published this material it would have been of great interest in the period before electronic devices displaced mechanical ones, and others might have been able to build on his work.

Babbage started working on the mechanical design of the Analytical Engine in 1834 and continued, with some intermission, for the rest of his life; even in his later years he was making progress in the directions of greater simplicity and greater efficiency. He began a series of successful experiments with an early form of die casting. One can understand that he was disinclined to publish while he felt he was still making progress. It is surprising, however, that he did not publish an early sketch which he wrote in 1837 and which bears all the signs of being intended for publication. It was written before Babbage had become immersed in detail and gives a very clear outline of what the Analytical Engine would have been like.

Babbage proposed to control his machine by means of punched cards strung together as in an automatic loom and behaving very much like punched paper tape. However, anyone who expects to find that Babbage anticipated modern ideas in detail will be disappointed. For example, although he numbered the locations in his store, he could not increment these numbers or otherwise modify them in ways now familiar. Moreover, he had independently stepped card mechanisms to control the passage of variables to and from the store and to control the mill, as he called his arithmetical unit. He never arrived at the idea, so obvious to us, of associating an operation code permanently with the name of a variable on the same card. Nevertheless, he had the concept of loops in the program, and he recognized that a set of cards for his engine would constitute a representation of an algorithm.[1]

For lower level control, Babbage devised a system very similar to modern microprogramming with rotating barrels carrying projecting studs taking the place of the read-only memory. The studs controlled the action of the various parts of the machine and could also cause the barrel to step forward or backwards by any desired amount. Babbage prepared notations, as he called them, for the execution of a variety of algorithms and many of these still exist. Their resemblance to modern microprograms is very close and shows that Babbage thoroughly understood what we would call the art of microprogramming.

Not unnaturally, Babbage had some difficulty in communicating to his contemporaries the full breadth of his vision. Towards the end of his life, he wrote that, if any man "unwarned by my example," should ever succeed in building an Analytical Engine "I have no fear of leaving my reputation in his charge, for he alone will be fully able to appreciate the nature of my efforts and the value of their results." Truer words than these have never been written. It was only when the first digital computers had come into action that the extent of Babbage's genius became fully appreciated.

Babbage's Private Life and Personality

Babbage's intense emotional involvement with the Difference Engine started early. In February 1829 William Whewell—who was two years junior to Babbage and himself destined to achieve distinction—writes in a letter to a friend that Babbage's "anxiety about the success and fame of his machine is quite devouring and unhappy." He never admitted that the idea was not as good as he thought it was, and his feeling of resentment against the scientific establishment of the day amounted at times almost to a persecution mania. This feeling did not, however, flow over into his social life, which was a great success. One senses a certain awkwardness in his dealings with people, but he must also have been a man of great charm. He knew everyone and went everywhere. Carriages crowded the street outside his house when his Saturday evening parties were in progress.[2]

3 *Babbage's grave in Kensal Green cemetery, London. The photograph was taken on 26 December 1991, the 200th anniversary of Babbage's birth, by James Roberts. It shows the author (standing), with Allan Bromley of the University of Sydney, who is well known for his researches on Babbage. The gravestone, of polished granite, is of simple design and contrasts sharply with the elaborate nature of other monuments near it.*

Full and successful as his social life was, Babbage was lonely in his private life. After thirteen years of very happy married life, he had the misfortune to lose his wife and two children in a short space, having lost his father very shortly before. He was long in recovering from this blow. Of eight children, three sons only survived into adult life. A daughter of whom he was very fond died at the age of seventeen. All three sons followed careers overseas. His eldest son, Herschel, went to work on the Continent with Brunel and then migrated permanently to South Australia, where he became an important man in the colony. The youngest son, Henry, went into the military service of the East India Company.

The middle son, Dugald, was not as successful in life as his brothers. He also went to South Australia. He was somewhat disapproved of by his brother Herschel for mixing with his social inferiors and being too fond, so Herschel said, of a glass of wine.[3] I find my heart warming towards Dugald. To me he seems the most human member of that family of earnest Victorians.

References

Airy, Wilfrid, ed. *Autobiography of Sir George Biddle Airy*. Cambridge: University Press, 1896.

Babbage, Charles. *Passages from the Life of a Philosopher*. London: Spon, 1864. Reprint, London: Dawwsons, 1968; also, London: Pickering, 1994.

Bromley, Allan G. "Charles Babbage's Analytical Engine, 1838." *Ann. Hist. Comp.*, vol. 4, no. 3 (1982), pp. 196–217.

Bromley, Allan G. "The Evolution of Babbage's Calculating Engines." *Ann. Hist. Comp.*, vol. 9, no. 2 (1987), pp. 113–36.

Campbell-Kelly, Martin, ed. *The Works of Charles Babbage*, 11 vols. London: Pickering and Chatto, 1989.

Hyman, Anthony. *Charles Babbage, Pioneer of the Computer*. Princeton: Princeton University Press, 1982.

Morrison, Philip and Emily Morrison. *Charles Babbage and His Calculating Machines*. New York: Dover Publications, 1961 (currently out of print).

Wilkes, Maurice V. "Babbage's Expectations for his Engines." *Ann. Hist. Comp.*, vol. 13, no. 2 (1991), pp. 141–46.

Wilkes, Maurice V. "Pray, Mr. Babbage . . . A Character Study in Dramatic Form." *Ann. Hist. Comp.*, vol. 13, no. 2 (1991), pp. 147–54.

ESSAY TWO

The Beginnings of Electronic Computers

Although computers began to appear less than fifty years ago, people have been computing for a very long time, both for business and scientific purposes. Traditionally most scientific computing was done by astronomers, but they were joined in the earlier part of this century by statisticians and other scientists.

Most business accounting and scientific computing was done on desk calculating machines. Punched card accounting machines, although expensive and inflexible, were making steady progress for large, routine jobs. Analog machines—which were intended for scientific computation only—had a short-lived impact.

Desk machines have a history going back to Pascal, at least; modern pocket calculators are their direct lineal descendants. Although effective desk calculating machines existed in the nineteenth century, they did not come into general use, either in business or science, until the 1920s. Up until that time most calculation had been done mentally, except that logarithms were used in astronomy and other subjects in which trigonometrical functions were involved. L. J. Comrie, who became a leader in the development of scientific computing, records that when he joined

4 *The Harvard Mark I computer. In front, from left to right are Howard H. Aiken, Grace Hopper, and Robert V. D. Campbell, who appear in Naval uniform, the machine being then operated under the auspices of the U.S. Navy. After the war, all three reverted to civilian status on the staff of the Computation Laboratory, with Howard Aiken as Director. Grace Hopper later joined Eckert and Mauchly on the UNIVAC project and became well known for her work on the standardization of Cobol. She remained on the Naval Reserve, and in 1971 returned to active duty, retiring at the age of 80 with the rank of Rear Admiral.* (Courtesy of Harvard University Archives.)

the British Nautical Almanac Office in 1925 logarithms were still being used. By the 1930s, with the development of improved desk machines and improved computing techniques, numerical methods, although slow and laborious, were proving very powerful in such subjects as quantum theory, wave propagation, structures, etc.

Mathematical tables were important tools for users of desk calculating machines—almost as important as the machines themselves. The British Association Mathematical Tables Committee had over a long period of time played a leading role in their computation and publication.

When I joined the Committee in 1939, I found that very sophisticated and highly mechanized procedures were in use. Of special importance was the Class 3000 National Accounting Machine which Comrie had shown could be used both for differencing and sub-tabulation. Differences were important for various reasons, but particularly because they enabled errors, including blunders made by an operator, to be detected.[4] Sub-tabulation enabled a table to be computed with a wide interval in the argument and subsequently broken down to a smaller interval.

Large-Scale Computing Machinery Before 1945

The machines used in scientific calculation were almost without exception machines which had been developed for office work. This remained true of desk calculating machines, but in the late 1930s and early 1940s a number of projects were in progress for the development of large-scale automatic computing machinery. The Bell Telephone Laboratories produced several machines, based on telephone relays, for interpolation and complex number calculations and began to embark on the construction of a fully automatic computer. At Harvard, the Automatic Sequence Controlled Calculator (usually known as Harvard Mark I) was built by IBM engineers according to the proposals of Professor Howard Aiken. This machine used technology from IBM punched card accounting machines. It was running in 1944. In Germany, Konrad Zuse was responsible for some pioneering developments but these, being for a long time quite unknown in the United States and the United Kingdom, were without the influence that they might otherwise have had.

The above machines had very limited storage and primitive control mechanisms. They were mechanical in action and therefore very slow. They were soon to be rendered obsolete by the development of electronic machines. Nevertheless they were notable achievements in their time and they gave their users a taste of what was to come.

The ENIAC

The first large-scale automatic electronic computing machine was the ENIAC, built in Philadelphia at the Moore School of Electrical Engineering of the University of Pennsylvania. The ENIAC was operating in 1945. It was the brainchild and practical creation of two remarkable engineers, Presper Eckert and John Mauchly. It was designed for numerical calculation and sponsored by the U.S. Ordnance Department, which proposed to use it for the calculation of artillery firing tables. It was in no sense a modern computer, but it was a harbinger of the modern computer. It showed beyond any doubt that the use of vacuum tubes in large numbers was viable.

When the construction of the ENIAC was reaching completion, Eckert and Mauchly had the leisure to make a reappraisal. The ENIAC was a dinosaur; it contained more than 18,000 vacuum tubes. It had been designed in a very straightforward way by taking mechanical features such as counter wheels and translating them into electronic terms. Eckert and Mauchly realized that a more radical and logical approach would enable a much more powerful machine to be built with a fraction of the equipment. In particular Eckert realized, very clearly, the importance of storage, not only for numbers but for the program as well. The ENIAC was programmed by putting plugs into sockets and setting up a myriad of switches. Eckert recognized that this was nothing more than a way—an inconvenient way—of storing a program.

During September 1944, Eckert and Mauchly were joined by John von Neumann, a well-known mathematician of the period. The group already included Herman Goldstine and Arthur Burks, also mathematicians. The discussions that took place in the augmented group were very lively, as anyone who knew both von Neumann and Eckert would have expected. From the discussions there rapidly crystalized a package of ideas that has formed the basis of subsequent electronic computer development. It consisted partly of new ideas and partly of old ideas reasserted in the new setting.

The ideas may be summarized as follows:

Electronic operation: vacuum tubes would be used for everything except input and output.

Binary: even if the machine appeared from the outside to be a decimal one, inside it would be composed of binary elements.

Instruction set as user interface: the problem was to be specified by writing a program composed of instructions taken from a well-defined set; no setting up of plug boards or switches

5 *A photograph of the ENIAC taken shortly after its completion at the Moore School of Electronic Engineering in Philadelphia. The program was set up on the machine by means of a system of cables with plugs and sockets; some of the cables can be seen in the photograph. In addition a large number of switches had to be correctly set. On the extreme right is the IBM punched card equipment used for input and output. The operators are setting numbers on arrays of rotary switches. These were known as function tables and acted as read-only memories.*

(Courtesy of Charles Babbage Institute, University of Minnesota.)

was to be necessary. This required that the instruction set should contain instructions for organizing the flow of control as well as for performing arithmetic and logical operations.

Serial execution of instructions: instructions were to be executed one at a time, those concerned with the organization of the flow of control taking their turn with those calling for arithmetic operations.

Single memory: the memory would contain addressable words each composed of the same number of binary digits; addresses would consist of integers running consecutively through the memory. If a word were sent to the control unit it would be interpreted as an instruction, and if sent to the arithmetic unit it would be interpreted as an item of data.

Modification and construction of instructions: the programmer would be able to modify addresses, or indeed whole instructions, by performing arithmetical or logical operations on them in the arithmetic unit. Similarly, he would have the power to construct new instructions and plant them in a program.

The last three items constitute the stored program principle which, when used as a term of art, means something more than that the program is stored in a memory.

It is not always that the historian can pinpoint, as closely as in this case, the source of ideas that have changed the world, and one would prefer not to have to try to allocate credit between members of the Moore School group. Unfortunately, there has been a long-standing tendency to give the whole credit to von Neumann. This was originally because the ideas first became known outside the Moore School through a draft of a report prepared by von Neumann and bearing his name only. It is regrettable that the term "von Neumann computer" has obtained currency. I prefer to use the term "Eckert–von Neumann computer," although I am conscious that this still does an injustice to Mauchly and, to a lesser extent, to the other members of the group.

The principles that I have just set out led to the design of a computer that would be both simple and elegant. It would contain a fraction of the number of vacuum tubes to be found in the ENIAC and would, at the same time, be much more powerful. This improvement in cost-effectiveness was obtained by rationalizing the use of memory and by reducing the amount of special equipment associated with a particular function and incapable of being used for any other purpose. For example, no special equipment would be provided for executing loops in the program; the instruction set provided all that was necessary for the establishment of loops, and the programmer would have the power of modifying instructions in the arithmetic unit (later computers were to provide index registers for this purpose). There would be no special provision for tables; the tabular values would be stored in the memory like any other numbers, and a program would be used for interpolation. Similarly, binary/decimal conversion needed no special provision, since it could be done by program. The rationalization of memory leads to great economy since it is obviously better to have a single large memory in which space can be allocated for different purposes as the exigencies of the moment indicate, than to have a number of separate memories dedicated to particular functions.

Something was paid in speed for the simplification which the adoption of the stored program principle led to. In particular, using instructions from the instruction set for the purpose of organizing the calculation meant that for a good deal of its time the computer was engaged on administrative tasks, rather than in doing useful computation. In a mechanical computer this would have been only too obvious to the bystander and if Babbage had hit on the stored program principle, he would undoubtedly have rejected it for that reason. With electronics, what the eye does not see, the heart does not grieve over.

References

Ralston, Anthony and Edwin D. Reilly, eds. *Encyclopedia of Computer Science*, 3rd ed. New York: Van Nostrand Reinhold, 1993. [Contains articles on early machines, including the Harvard Mark I, the Bell Telephone Laboratories machines, the Zuse machines, and the ENIAC.]

Comrie, L.J. "Inverse Interpolation and Scientific Applications of the National Accounting Machine." *J. Royal Statistical Soc.*, vol. 3, suppl. (1936), p. 87.

Massey, H.W. "L.J. Comrie." *Obituary Notices of Fellows of the Royal Society of London*, vol. 8, no. 21 (1952), p. 97.

ESSAY THREE

The Development of the Stored Program Computer

The brief and fruitful interval in which engineers and mathematicians could put their heads together and evolve the ideas set out in the previous essay was soon over. The ideas, once evolved, were clear and complete and there was nothing further for the mathematicians to contribute. However, the task was just beginning for engineers.

At the end of 1946 various organizations were setting out to build computers. I will mention the more important. One of the groups was headed by Eckert and Mauchly, who had left the Moore School to found a company and build the UNIVAC. Another group was established by von Neumann at the Institute for Advanced Study, Princeton. In England, there were groups at Manchester University and at the National Physical Laboratory, as well as a group in Cambridge led by myself. Slightly later, the National Bureau of Standards (now the National Institute of Science and Technology) established two groups, one in Washington, D.C. and one in Los Angeles. By that time a group at MIT was working on the Whirlwind. All these groups eventually produced successful computers. It has been said that they engaged in a race to build the first computer. It did not appear that way at the time. Indeed, it would have been a funny

6 *Presper Eckert and John Mauchly, designers of the ENIAC, left the Moore School in 1946 to design and market the UNIVAC. This photograph was taken in 1951 when the first UNIVAC was being delivered to the U.S. Bureau of the Census, where it remained in use until 1963. Eckert is on the extreme left with Mauchly next to him.*

(Courtesy of Unisys.)

sort of race with the competitors making for different finishing points. At one extreme, our group in Cambridge, England, set out to build an effective machine that could be made available to programmers, and we had a relaxed attitude to performance; at the other extreme, Eckert and Mauchly were aiming to produce a marketable machine designed to the highest standards.

Electronic engineers who came to computer design, as I did, with a background in such subjects as ionosphere research and radar were accustomed to short pulses and wide bandwidths. They were used to thinking in terms of discrete pulses with time intervals between them, rather than in terms of Fourier components and phase differences, as was traditional in communication engineering. Nevertheless they had much to learn. Vacuum tubes are analog devices and the first task was to learn how to use them to construct digital switching and storage elements. The second was to learn how to design circuits that would handle transients correctly. In a radar set it does not matter if occasionally there is a flash on the screen, but a computer will make errors if pulses are mutilated. This and similar problems encountered in designing a computer may have come as a mild surprise, but they could be solved readily enough. Quite new was the design of a digital memory, since nothing of the kind had existed before.

As I have said, Eckert had realized that the basis of an efficient electronic computer would be a digital memory capable of holding thousands of bits. Eckert made the practical proposal that a workable memory could be based on an ultrasonic delay unit. This consists of a steel tube—the ones in the machine built at Cambridge University (the EDSAC) were about 5 feet long and 3/4 inch in internal diameter—filled with mercury. At each end is a quartz crystal. Electronic pulses are applied to one of the crystals with the result that ultrasonic waves are generated and travel down the column of mercury to the other end. Here they meet the second crystal, which reconverts them into electronic pulses. These pulses are amplified, reshaped, retimed, and passed back to the originating quartz crystal. Since several hundred pulses can be in transit down the tube at any time, one has, in effect, a memory system. Circuits must be provided to enable pulses to be inserted and retrieved when necessary. Building such a memory took one into unknown territory, but it was not to be regarded as high-risk research. Nevertheless, the EDSAC group felt very relieved when they had succeeded in demonstrating that a battery of ultrasonic tanks—as the tubes were called to avoid confusion with vacuum tubes—could be made to work satisfactorily and would hold pulses over long periods.

At the end of the war, F. C. Williams was experimenting in one of the U.K. radar establishments with a system of storage that made use of an ordinary cathode-ray tube, digits being stored in the form of a charge pattern on the back of the screen. He moved to Manchester University and took the work with him. This was indeed high-risk research, but it was brilliantly

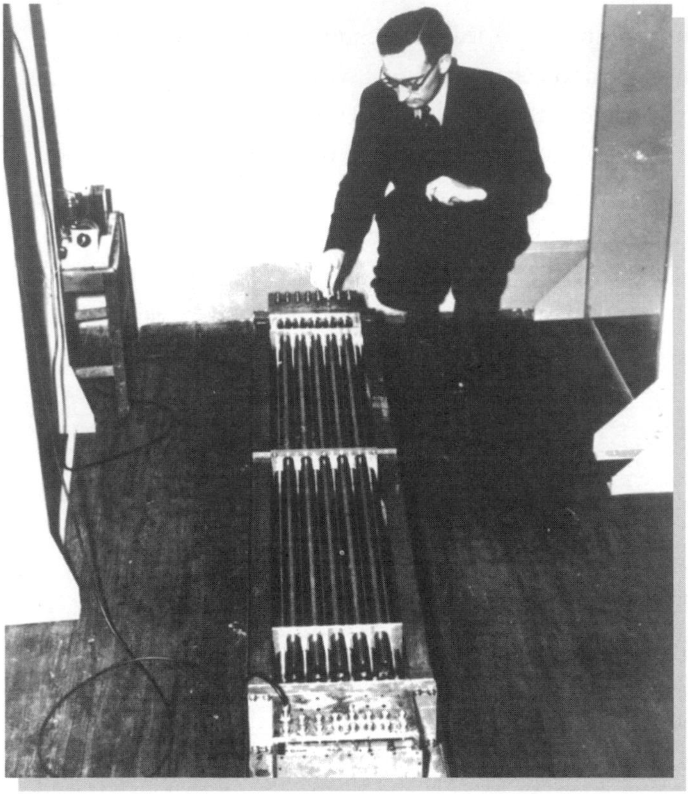

7 *This photograph, taken in 1947, shows the author with the first battery of mercury tanks, or ultrasonic delay units, built for the EDSAC. The battery contained 16 tanks (tubes), of which the top row of five can be seen. The metal box at the end nearer to the camera contains matching sections used to interface the quartz crystals at the ends of the tanks to the coaxial cables connecting them with the electronic chassis.*

(Courtesy of The Computer Museum, Boston.)

conducted and completely successful. With the help of his collaborator, T. Kilburn, he went on to exploit it by building a computer.

All the early machines used either ultrasonic or Williams tube memories, except the Whirlwind which had its own form of cathode-ray tube memory, working on different principles and using specially made tubes. As time went on the Williams tube memory was widely adopted. It was much faster than the ultrasonic memory and without it the computer field would have developed more slowly than it actually did. As a technology, however, the Williams tube did not survive long enough to become mature; by 1954 the early core memories were being constructed, and offered such significant advantages that they soon came into universal use. Core memories, in their turn, gave way to semiconductor memories in the 1970s. This short life cycle for a technology is one of the characteristics of the present age.

8 *The author (kneeling) with some of his colleagues in a posed group taken while the EDSAC was under construction. William Renwick, the principal engineer on the project, is in the rear facing a rack partly filled with electronic chassis.*

(Courtesy of The Computer Museum, Boston.)

Although the designers of the various early machines were facing essentially the same problems, there was a surprising variation in the circuit technology that they developed. The EDSAC, which was a serial machine, used AC coupling with DC restorers; vacuum tubes were used for amplification and vacuum diodes for switching. The SEAC, built by S. A. Alexander for the National Bureau of Standards in Washington, D.C., was also serial; it was designed, slightly later than the EDSAC, at a time when semiconductor (germanium) diodes had become available. It was in advance of its time in making use of small plug-in modules, each containing one vacuum tube amplifier and a number of diodes. The machine built at Princeton by J. Bigelow had a parallel architecture. It was DC coupled and used double grid tubes for switching. In spite of their differences, all of these approaches led to satisfactory machines. The important thing was consistency and careful design.

There was an uneasy interval of some three to four years before the new machines were ready for testing. In retrospect this does not seem very long but at the time it seemed interminable. A real need for computing power began to be felt and a number of devices of limited capacity, such as the IBM Card Programmed Calculator and the IBM 604, enjoyed a certain success. They were, however, rapidly swept away when stored program computers became available.

The Seminal Years

The years around 1960 were seminal years, particularly as regards what we now call software. To those years we owe high-level languages, operating systems, timesharing, and computer graphics, although the antecedents of all these developments may be traced back earlier.

This progress was possible because computers had become large enough and reliable enough for programmers to give full rein to their inventiveness. Moreover, a solution had been found to a problem that had been felt, to a greater or less degree, in many important application

9 *The author holding one of the electronic chassis used in conjunction with the mercury tank battery shown in Figure 7 on page 24. One such chassis was associated with each tank in the battery. The photograph was taken in 1982 in the Computer Museum, then located in Marlborough, Massachusetts.*

(Courtesy of The Computer Museum, Boston.)

areas. This arose from the fact that the only available form of storage for data in bulk was on magnetic tape. While magnetic tape was satisfactory for applications in which data could be processed serially, its long latency time made it impossibly slow when random access was required. The solution was the development of the disk file, the first of which, the IBM RAMAC, was announced in 1956. Early disk files were large and cumbersome, and their capacity left much to be desired (see Figure 17 on page 57). The steady progress made in disk technology—a progress that still continues—has been every bit as remarkable as that made in semiconductors.

Oddly enough, although computers were all the time becoming faster and more reliable, these years were ones of great turmoil for computer engineers, since transistors were coming in to replace vacuum tubes. The engineers had to forget everything they knew about circuit design and start learning afresh. They were not helped by the fact that the early transistors were a good deal more awkward to use in digital circuits than vacuum tubes had been. It reflects great credit on the designers of the period that the transition to transistors was made so smoothly. It was as though the foundations of a cathedral were being wholly renewed, while services were going on in the choir and the organ was playing.

The Software Avalanche

Perhaps the most striking feature of the computer age has been the headlong rush of software progress. This has been fed, indeed driven, by continual hardware innovation. However, the software avalanche could not even have started if it had not been for certain features of the stored program computer which have already been mentioned.

The first was the wholehearted adoption of the serial principle. The Harvard Mark II—the second machine to be built at Harvard—had an adder and two multipliers. It was a pain in the neck for the programmer to keep all these busy at the same time. As I remarked above, there was some loss of speed consequent on doing everything serially. The gain in simplicity of use was, however, so great that no one wanted to go back. It is not too much to say that the adoption of serial execution of a single instruction stream made possible the development of modern software with its layer upon layer of complexity. In due course, the hardware began to get back some of the lost speed by the use of pipelining and other techniques that enabled the

10 *Part of a Williams tube memory, developed at Manchester University in England, by F. C. Williams and T. Kilburn. Binary digits are stored in the form of patterns of electric charge on the inner surface of the screen of a cathode ray tube enclosed in a screening can. The hinged end plate carries a circular electrode which, in the working position, is in contact with the front of the tube and picks up signals by induction as the spot sweeps across the screen. Not shown are the electronic circuits for writing, reading, and periodically regenerating the stored information.*

(Courtesy of The Computer Museum, Boston.)

execution of instructions to be overlapped. This was, however, done behind the back of the programmer, who continued to write programs in serial form.

The second feature that has made the software avalanche possible is that computers are able to help with the preparation and editing of their own programs. This is possible because instructions can be constructed or modified in the arithmetic unit. Explicit modification of addresses by orders included in the program for the purpose ceased to be necessary with the introduction of index registers. However, the ability to construct orders remains of prime importance. The first application of this ability was the conversion of instructions to binary form. Another application was the writing of an interpreter so that a computer could execute

II *Generations of technology used in IBM machines: vacuum tubes used in the 700 series, discrete transistors used in the 1401, Solid Logic Technology, a form of hybrid technology used in the 360 series, and (in the foreground), integrated circuits with an average of six circuits per chip introduced for the 370 series.*

(Courtesy of International Business Machines, Inc.)

instructions, such as floating-point instructions, that did not appear in its instruction set. Finally, it made compilers possible. Programs could then be written in a high-level language and run on any computer that had the appropriate compiler. Programs in fact became independent, free-standing artifacts with an existence of their own. It was not long before mathematicians became interested in proving things about them.

The property that makes these things possible is the property of universality. A machine possessing this property is capable of emulating any other machine. In 1937, Turing, in a famous paper, described a machine now known as the Turing machine which had this property. It was a purely theoretical concept and was used to prove an important theorem in mathematical logic. There is no hint in the paper that the Turing machine might have any connection with practical computing machinery. Among real machines the stored program computer has the property of universality—subject to a physical limitation on the amount of storage that can be supplied—but no monopoly of the property. Arguments can be put forward to show that all sorts of unlikely machines are universal machines. However, in general this is an intellectual exercise only, since either the inefficiency would be too great for the property to be useful or there would be too severe a limitation on the maximum storage that could be provided. The important point is that the modern stored program computer—the Eckert–von Neumann computer—is efficient enough for the property of universality to be useful.

References

Ralston, Anthony and Edwin. D. Reilly, eds. *Encyclopedia of Computer Science*, 3rd ed. New York: Van Nostrand Reinhold, 1993.

Turing, A.M. "On Computable Numbers, with an Application to the Entscheidungsproblem." *Proc. Lond. Math. Soc.*, series 2, vol 42 (1937), pp. 230–65.

von Neumann, John. "First Draft of a Report on the EDVAC." Moore School of Electrical Engineering, University of Pennsylvania, 1945. Reprinted in *Origins of Digital Computers: Selected Papers*, ed. Brian Randell. Berlin: Springer-Verlag, 1982. Also reprinted in *Papers of Von Neumann on Computing and Computing Theory*, vol. 12, Charles Babbage Institute Reprint Series for the History of Computing. Cambridge: MIT Press, 1986.

PART TWO

Processor Technology and Workstations

ESSAY FOUR

Personal Computers and Workstations

It is tempting for computer scientists to trace the development of personal computers to the Alto developed at the Palo Alto Research Center of the Xerox Corporation (Xerox PARC). It is quite true that the pioneering work started at Xerox PARC in 1972 on the use of personal computers and servers connected to an ethernet had a profound effect on the development of that style of computing. However, the hardware developments that led to personal computers being made and sold in large numbers from the mid 1970s onwards had nothing to do with Xerox PARC. Microprocessors were not a product of the computer industry at all. They were the outcome of the desire—and the imperative need—of the young semiconductor industry to find a profitable application for early VLSI when only a few thousand transistors could be put on a chip.[5]

The story begins with the Intel 4004, which was a pocket calculator chip designed by Ted Hoff for Busicom, a Japanese company. Hoff's proposal for a programmable device was preferred on the grounds of economy to an original proposal for a special-purpose, non-programmable device. The 4004 comprised about 2,300 transistors. It was a 4-bit device, as was appropriate for

12 *The Alto computer developed at the Palo Alto Research Center of the Xerox Corporation (PARC) in the early 1970s. On the desk is a tray containing disk cartridges. When a user inserted his own disk cartridge into any Alto, that Alto became personalized to his use. Research done at PARC with the Alto laid the foundations of client-server computer systems long before the modern low cost personal computers based on VLSI became available.*

binary coded decimal operation. It was made generally available—that is, not only available to Busicom—in 1971.

In April 1972 came the Intel 8008, which comprised 3,300 transistors. This was sponsored by a company planning a terminal, although in fact, it turned out to be too slow for that application. The 8008 was an 8-bit device suitable for ASCII applications.

The Reinvention of the Computer

The Intel enginers knew little about computer architecture. Their immediate objective was to make programmable devices that would replace random logic. What they ended by doing was to reinvent the digital computer. Like the embryo in the womb, microprocessors went through all the stages of evolution of the digital computer, but faster.

Given the 4004 it was possible to play at making a personal computer; with the 8008 it was possible to do so more seriously. The challenge was taken up in the United States by people who were not computer scientists or software engineers. They were amateurs with no previous reputation at all. They heard about the Intel 4004 and the amateur movement began. It is, I think, right to call it a movement, like women's lib or opposition to nuclear power. For those involved it was a time of excitement, anticipation, and fulfillment. Computers were lashed up on kitchen tabletops and, as time went on, companies were started, not for good business reasons, but because friends or friends of friends wanted copies of those computers. Few of the companies survived.

I was living in England when the movement grew up, and the view that I have just presented is one given me by an American friend who saw it all happen. He was thinking of the personal computers themselves, rather than of the microprocessor chips on which they were based. Others would stress the role of young people with strong links with university laboratories like my old laboratory, the Computer Laboratory in Cambridge, England. However, they did not come into it until later.

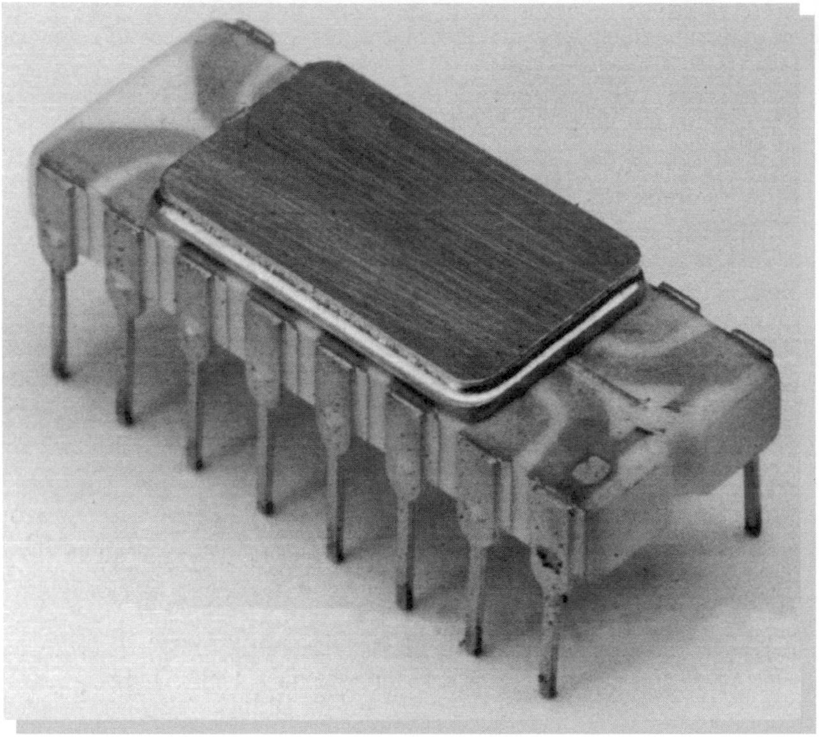

13 *The Intel 4004 marketed in 1971. It contained about 2,300 transistors and was the starting point from which Intel developed the early single chip microprocessors.*

(Courtesy of Intel Corporation.)

In April 1974 Intel announced the 8080, which had 4,500 transistors. This was not aimed simply at logic replacement and looked much more like a digital computer. In January 1978 a kit based on it was offered, namely the MITS Altair 8800. This had an open-bus architecture and an operating system, namely CP/M. The bus ultimately became the IEEE 696. Some people would say that the Altair 8800 is the true ancestor of the modern personal computer.

In reply Motorola introduced the 6800. This was designed by Chuck Peddle, who shortly afterwards moved to MOS Technology for whom he designed the 6502, which was announced in September 1975. The 6502 was sold at a low price and formed the basis of many personal computers—Atari, Commodore Pet, BBC Micro, Apple, and others. At about this point Federico Faggin, who had played a major role at Intel in making the 4004 work, founded Zilog. In 1976 Zilog announced the Z80. This had an instruction set similar to that of the 8080, but with some enhancements; it was faster and it supported dynamic RAM. The ZX80 announced by Clive Sinclair in February 1980 was based on the Z80. This was one of the first computers to be produced in large quantities and sold at a low price. When my wife and I were about to move to the United States in September 1980 we gave a farewell party. Some of the guests brought flowers for my wife; it was a sign of the times that Sinclair should bring a ZX80 computer for me.

From Personal Computers to Workstations

In 1979 Motorola released the 68000; this was a 16-bit processor, but internally had 32-bit registers. Earlier microprocessors had been hard wired, but the 68000 was microprogrammed.[6] The 68000 was a very successful processor and was chosen by Apple for the Macintosh. It was used in personal computers marketed by Apollo and also by Sun and Hewlett-Packard before they changed to RISC designs. These computers were more powerful than the traditional personal computer, and were of interest to a much wider range of users, including users who, up to that time, had relied on central services provided by large minicomputers. Personal computers in this class were to become known as workstations. The power of the 68000 may be put into perspective by saying that it was a little faster than the Alto developed at Xerox PARC for in-house use, but less powerful than the Dorado developed later.

It is interesting to observe that both the Motorola 68000 and the Intel 80286—known for short as the 286—and more powerful processors based on them have continued to play a major

14 *The MITS Altair 8800. Based on the Intel 8080, which contained 4,500 transistors, the Altair 8800 was marketed in kit form, and may be regarded as the ancestor of today's personal computers.*

(Courtesy of The Computer Museum, Boston.)

role in personal computers up to the present time (1994). The 286, in particular, has gone through a remarkable series of upgrades as semiconductor process technology has advanced. First there was the 386, and then the 486. For commercial reasons, the latest processor in the series, announced in 1993, is called the Pentium, not, as might have been expected, the 586. The native operating system for the whole range is MS-DOS, written in assembly language. However, the more powerful ones are capable of running UNIX and can then be classed as workstations. These chips have thus carried the IBM PC—and its many copies—from being a desktop computer of modest performance to being a powerful workstation.

Other processor chips appeared but, for various reasons, did not enjoy the same success in personal computers. However, the success of a processor chip, from the point of view of a semiconductor manufacturer, is not to be judged solely by the scale on which it is used in personal computers and workstations. Even more important to semiconductor companies, because of the large volumes required, is the market for embedded processors, that is, for processors to be incorporated in consumer products such as automobiles and washing machines, and in microcontrollers for industry.

References

Faggin, F. "The Birth of the Microprocessor." *Byte*, vol. 17, no. 3 (1992), pp. 145–50.

Garetz, M. "Evolution of the Microprocessor." *Byte*, vol. 10, no. 9 (1985), pp. 209–15.

Goldberg, Adele, ed. *A History of Personal Workstations*. New York: ACM Press, 1988. [This volume is a collection of revised versions of papers presented at the ACM Conference on the History of Personal Workstations held in January 1986.]

Williams, G. and M. Welch. "A Microcomputing Timeline." *Byte*, vol. 10, no. 9 (1985), p. 198–207.

ESSAY FIVE

The RISC Movement in Processor Architecture

The public debate which led to the RISC movement began with the publication, in the May 1980 issue of *Computer Architecture News*, of a paper by David Patterson and David Ditzel entitled "The Case for the Reduced Instruction Set Computer." It is from this paper that the acronym RISC derives. During the following year, papers began to appear on specific RISC designs. There was the Berkeley RISC Project, known as RISC I, described by Patterson and C.H. Séquin, and the Stanford MIPS Project described by John Hennessy. There was also a paper entitled "The 801 Minicomputer" by G. Radin of IBM. Radin mentioned that this project had started within IBM in 1975 and he gave an acknowledgement to John Cocke for the seminal idea.

The term "reduced instruction set" is not a wholly happy one. In using it, Patterson and Ditzel had in mind the VAX and other contemporary minicomputers which had very complex instruction sets, including elaborate addressing modes and other embellishments. It was compared to these computers that the proposed RISC instruction set was "reduced." Compared to computers designed at an earlier period, before microprogramming had gone to designers' heads, the RISC instruction set was not particularly small.

It is the style of the instruction set that is characteristic of RISC, rather than its size. However, size is also important. Every time a new instruction is added to an instruction set, the implementation becomes more complex. There is a danger that increased capacitative loading on gates in the critical path will make it necessary to reduce the clock rate. If this happens, the slowing down of the machine on each and every instruction may outweigh the gain achieved by including the new instruction. In early RISC literature, this argument for a simple instruction set was referred to as the "n+1 argument."

Characterization of a RISC Computer

A typical RISC computer contains a register file—commonly containing 16 or 32 registers—and an ALU, in which arithmetic and logical operations can be performed. Instructions fall mainly into two classes: (1) instructions which transfer words from the memory to a register or from a register to the memory, and (2) instructions which pass words from one or two of the registers through the ALU and put the result back into a register. In the case of instructions in the latter class, the operation itself, as distinct from the decoding of the instruction and disposing of the result, can be completed in a single clock cycle.

Floating-point operations are performed in a separate unit. VLSI lends itself to the implementation of highly parallel circuits and the floating-point units to be found in RISC computers are capable of performing a multiplication in a small number of clock cycles; usually, they are fully pipelined and capable of delivering a new result in every clock cycle.

A RISC instruction set is simple enough to be readily implemented without a microprogram. This is an advantage in itself, since hard-wiring is always faster. A weakness, recognized from the beginning, is that the density of code in a RISC computer is inevitably less than in a conventional computer. In other words, RISC programs take up more space in the memory. This is of little importance as far as the use of extra memory space is concerned, since far more space is commonly taken up by data than by code. More important is the fact that instruction access consumes more memory bandwidth. Early RISC designers did not allow density of code to worry them unduly, but current designers are more concerned about it. The secret of achieving good code density in a RISC computer, as in other computers, is to pay attention to the efficiency with which bits in an instruction are used. Inevitably, in some instructions, there will be bits or combinations of bits which are unused; the aim must be to reduce to a minimum the inefficiency arising from this cause. The issue is a complex one, involving consideration of instruction length, the number of bits required to specify an operation, and the number of registers in the register file.

The RISC Vision

The engineers who pioneered the RISC movement had one advantage over their predecessors who designed the earlier instruction sets. In the interval, simulation techniques had matured, and the computer power needed for their exploitation had become readily available. It became possible to assess the efficiency of a design without actually implementing it and to compare competing designs. In this way, the designer's intuition was replaced by measurement. It soon became apparent that unaided intuition was a very poor guide.

The conclusion drawn from early studies with a simulator was that a RISC processor would be half the size of a conventional processor, implemented with the same technology, and could be designed in half the time or less. Moreover, it would run at something like twice the speed.

I saw the early RISC development from within DEC, where I was working at the time. In 1983, Forest Baskett joined the company and set to work to build a RISC minicomputer using the fastest ECL MSI parts then available. This computer, known as the Titan, began to work in

1985, and confirmed the predictions that had been made by simulation. Soon RISC projects began to spring up in various parts of DEC.

At this time CMOS, as a process technology, was making great advances. Farsighted people were able to make the extrapolation that, in a very few years, VLSI CMOS would be the process of choice for high-speed computers. This was very clear to Patterson and Séquin and to Hennessy when they designed the Berkeley RISC and the Stanford MIPS, respectively. They saw themselves designing computers that would go on a single chip, but would at the same time achieve the sort of performance that was being achieved by contemporary minicomputers. Up to that time, single-chip microcomputers had been good for the PC market, but were not powerful enough to interest users of minicomputers. There was, on the contrary, nothing "micro" about the early integrated circuit RISC designs, except their physical size.

CMOS fulfilled the expectations that were based on it. Already in 1990, the DecStation 5000 (a workstation based on the MIPS R3000), announced in March of that year, had outperformed the Titan. By the end of 1993, CMOS RISC processors had overtaken all but the fastest supercomputers, and they still have a good way to go.

The RISC Achievement

In retrospect, the RISC movement was a child of its times. It was not, as some have mistakenly thought, a return to primitive purity and a rediscovery of forgotten principles. It was based, as I have emphasized, on a quantitative approach to performance evaluation, which in turn was made possible by the development of powerful simulation techniques. These techniques, in their turn, were made possible by the ready availability of computing power on a scale that was unthought of at an earlier period.

When main memories were slower than they are now, it was a sound strategy to pack as much information as possible into each instruction and to unpick it in the microprogram. As the gap in speed between microprogram memory and main memory decreased, this strategy became less effective. This was one of the reasons for the success of the RISC approach. More important, however, was the use in RISC processors of pipelining, a technique formerly found only in large computers. The original RISC processors had a pipeline with three stages. If that pipeline could have been kept constantly full, a gain in speed by a factor of three compared with a non-pipelined processor would have resulted. In practice a gain of around two was achieved. Now, of course, RISC processors have pipelines with more than three stages, and designers are looking to see what other techniques can be exploited for achieving parallelism at the level of the instruction set.

The early CMOS RISC designers were severely limited by the amount of silicon space available. It was not enough for them to consider whether a particular feature would, by itself, enhance performance; they had also to consider whether the space that it would occupy could not better be used in some other way. Extra cache memory was always a strong competitor for space. There was a time at which it could be said that a lean processor and a large cache was an unbeatable combination. The pressure on space is not now so intense, and it is possible to consider more favorably architectural enhancements that may give additional speed. However, intuition remains a dangerous guide, and it is an unwise designer who will take shortcuts with simulation.

Simulation techniques were also becoming more important for another reason, in addition to that mentioned above. When transistors were relatively slow, it was switching time, rather than interconnect time, that determined the speed at which hardware would operate. It was therefore possible to make speed measurements on an experimental model that could be rapidly and cheaply constructed with little regard being paid to the length of the interconnecting wires. As interconnect time became more and more a major factor, this was no longer possible, and reliable speed measurements could only be made on a prototype closely resembling the final product. In other words, it was no longer possible to separate physical design from circuit design.

References

Hennessy, J.L. and D.A. Patterson. *Computer Architecture: A Quantitative Approach*. San Francisco: Morgan Kaufmann, 1990.

Hennessy, J.L., N. Jouppi, F. Baskett, T. Gross, and J. Gill. "Hardware/Software Tradeoffs for Increased Performance." In Proc. Symp. on Architectural Support for Programming Languages and Operating Systems. *ACM Computer Architecture News*, vol. 10, no. 2 (1982), p. 2.

Patterson, D.A. and C.H. Séquin. "RISC I: A Reduced Instruction Set Computer." Proc. 8th Annual Symp. on Computer Architecture, *ACM Computer Architecture News,* vol. 9, no. 3 (1981), p. 443.

Katevenis, M.G.H. *Reduced Instruction Set Computer Architectures for VLSI*. Cambridge: MIT Press, 1986.

Radin, G. "The 801 Minicomputer." In Proc. Symp. on Architectural Support for Programming Languages and Operating Systems. *ACM Computer Architecture News*, vol. 10, no. 2 (1982), pp. 39–47. Reprinted in *IBM J. of Res. and Dev.*, vol. 27, no. 3 (1983), p. 237.

ESSAY SIX

Achievements and Challenges in VLSI Processor Design

In 1972, or thereabouts, when Intel found that they could put a primitive computer—consisting of a little over 3,000 transistors—on a single NMOS chip, the achievement went almost unnoticed in the computer industry. In retrospect, this may seem surprising, since the event may be said to mark the beginning of very large-scale integration, something which had been long heralded, but had been seemingly slow to come.

The reason for the lack of interest was partly that 2,000 transistors fell far short of what was needed to put a processor on a chip, and partly that the industry was fully occupied in exploiting medium-scale integration in the logic family known as TTL. TTL was based on bipolar transistors, and a wide range of parts, each containing a few logical elements—typically two flip-flops or up to sixteen gates in various combinations—were becoming available. TTL was highly successful. It was fast and versatile, and established new standards for cost-effectiveness and reliability. In 1972, NMOS seemed a step backwards as far as speed was concerned.

Microcomputers had a great success in the personal computer market which grew up alongside the older industry, and largely disconnected from it. Minicomputers were faster than microcomputers. With instruction sets of their own design and with proprietary software, manufacturers of minicomputers felt secure in their well-established markets. It was not until the mid 1980s that they began to come to terms with the idea that one day they might find themselves basing some of their products on microprocessors taken from the catalogues of semiconductor manufacturers, over whose instruction sets they had no control. They were even less prepared for the idea that personal computers, in an enhanced form known as workstations, would eventually come to challenge the traditional minicomputer. This is what has happened and a minicomputer is becoming nothing more than a workstation housed in a larger box, and provided with a wider range of peripheral and communication equipment.

The term "workstation" implies a computer that stands on a user's desk, or by the side of the desk, and is used by him or her personally. A workstation can, however, be as powerful as one of the older minicomputers or super-minicomputers and can be used in a similar role. For example, it can be used to provide a time-sharing service for a limited number of users, or as a server on a network. When used in these roles it may well have more disks and more peripherals, but it will still be essentially the same product. I like to call workstations used in this way "non-personal" workstations. The larger non-personal workstations take the place of minicomputers, but they cost less.

The simplicity of CMOS compared with ECL, along with low power consumption, made it possible for that technology to progress rapidly. In the last few years it has become the dominant technology for VLSI processors. Rapid shrinkage made CMOS competitive as regards speed with processors implemented in ECL at a lower scale of integration. That this would happen was predictable—and indeed was predicted by a few clear-sighted individuals—from the laws of physics. However, the progress to denser geometries has been much more rapid than could reasonably have been expected and the power of the resulting CMOS processors has taken the industry by surprise.

The speed at which CMOS rushed ahead is illustrated by the following dates. The Titan, DEC's first experimental RISC processor, was based on the fastest ECL technology then available, and was working in 1985. Five years later, in 1990, it was overtaken by a workstation based on a CMOS processor chip, namely the DECstation 5000.

The period was one of very rapid advance in a number of different areas: process technology; computer architecture (development of the RISC concept); accompanying development of compiler technology; simulation for logic verification and performance estimation; emergence of UNIX as a machine-independent operating system. The rapid development of process technology was particularly striking. It would be interesting to have an authoritative analysis of how it was that semiconductor engineers were able around 1987 to get their act together and move forward with a new confidence. No doubt a better understanding of the physical processes involved and advances in clean-room technology played their part. Perhaps also the industry, having tasted success, was prepared to invest more heavily in the future. Progress in CMOS technology continues unabated.

As soon as feature sizes of less than 1 micron had been achieved, it was realized that, for reasons of physics, a reduction in operating voltage would soon become necessary and fears were expressed that this might cause a hiccup in progress. However, this has not happened and progress continues to all appearances at the same rate as before. Again, it appeared that the passage from one layer of metal to several layers would present great process difficulties, mainly because of the unevenness of the chip surface by the time the lower layers had been deposited. Here, again, a solution was soon found to a problem that might have caused a serious holdup.

A Temporary Relaxation of Constraints

The new RISC processors naturally had non-standard instruction sets. According to the conventional wisdom of the time, this should have proved a fatal objection to their adoption. In fact, the emergence of UNIX as a machine-independent operating system neutralized this objection to an extent that many found surprising. As a result, the period was one of unusual freedom from compatibility constraints for the designer of workstations and the processor chips that go into them. The designer of a processor could choose an instruction set that would optimize performance. The writing of a C compiler provided compatibility with the world of UNIX workstations. More than one company took advantage of this freedom.

A Landmark Reached

In the middle of 1990, the MIPS R2000, or rather the R3000, a slightly shrunk version that followed very closely in time, represented the high-water mark of processor development. This chip contained a *basic RISC machine*, consisting of register file, ALU, and pipeline control. In addition, there was a memory management unit with its associated TLB, and also control circuits for data and instruction caches. The caches themselves were off-chip and so was the floating-point arithmetic unit. The high performance of this chip was due partly to the speed of the CMOS circuits, but there was also a significant bonus arising from the fact that the basic RISC machine, together with the other units mentioned above, were entirely on one chip, and time delays involved in sending signals from one chip to another were avoided. Being able to put all these circuits on the same chip represented a major landmark.

It is worth noting that on the R2000/3000 nearly half the space is occupied by the basic RISC machine. This takes up only half the space of a conventional processor. If it had not been for RISC, therefore, the above landmark would not have been reached until it became possible to put twice as many transistors on a chip. If one adopts the rule of thumb that the number doubles every two years, this would have meant two years' delay. At that critical moment, two years' delay could have had a significant effect on subsequent events in the computer industry.

The next step after the R3000 was clearly to bring the cache and floating-point unit onto the same chip, and it seemed that process technology was advancing at the right rate to

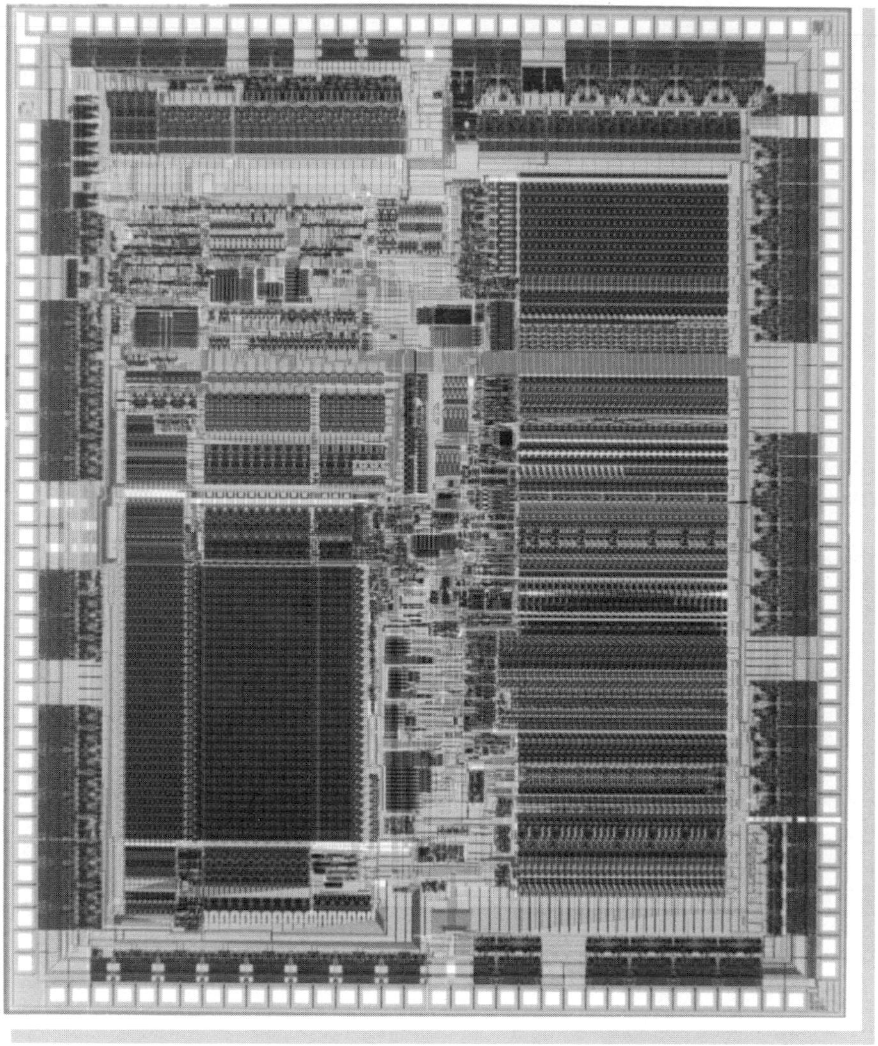

15 *The MIPS R2000/3000 processor chip developed in 1986. Without RISC technology, it would not have been possible to put a processor, a memory management unit (MMU), a translation look-aside buffer (TLB), and cache control circuits on the same chip, since a conventional processor would have occupied nearly all the chip. There were about 100,000 transistors on this chip.*

(Courtesy of MIPS Computer Systems, Inc.)

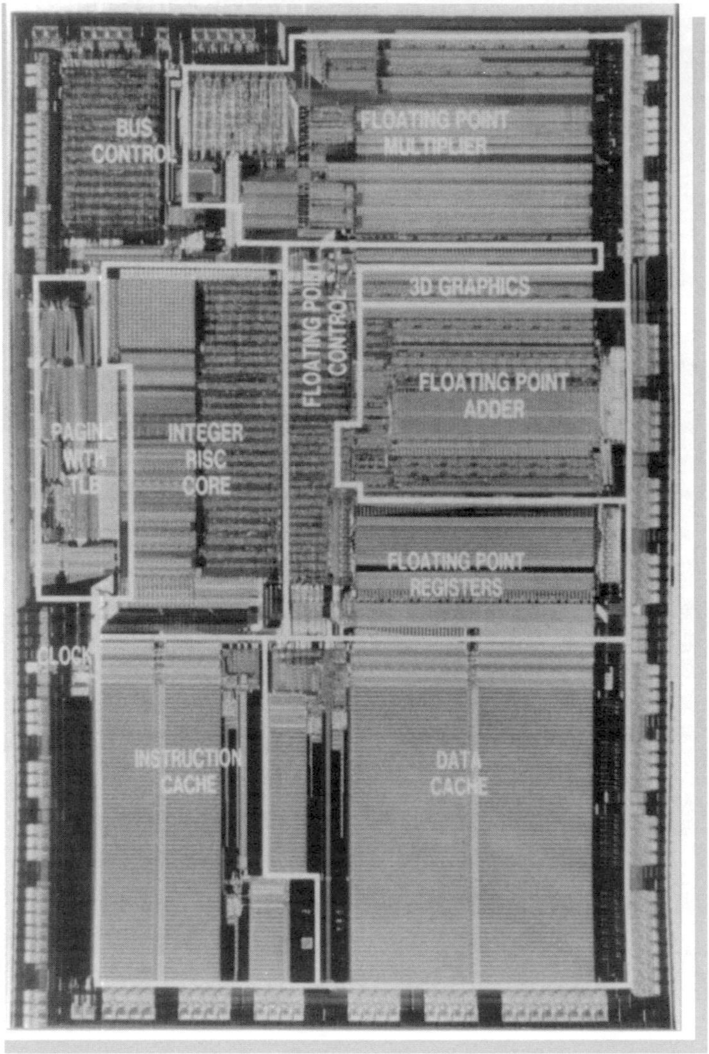

16 *The Intel i860 processor was developed three years after the MIPS R2000/3000 shown in Figure 15 and highlights the advances made in semiconductor technology. The silicon area is greater by a factor of slightly more than two and the line width less by a factor of 2.5. The basic RISC processor (integer RISC core) now occupies only a small part of the chip. There are two on-chip caches and an on-chip floating-point co-processor. Much of the extra space is used for memory, which is dense in transistors. This accounts for the fact that the total transistor count is ten times that of the MIPS chip, not five times as the above figures might suggest.* (Courtesy of Intel Corporation.)

make this possible in the near future. Two chips in the design stage that were of particular interest were the MIPS R4000 and the Intel i860.

The Intel i860 processor was developed three years after the MIPS R3000 and illustrates the progress that had taken place in process technology. The silicon area was greater by a factor of slightly more than 2, and the amount of space occupied by a transistor less by a factor of 2.5. This gave a fivefold effective increase in the space available. The space occupied by the basic RISC processor itself is only 10% of the whole as compared with 50% on the R2000. About 38% is used for the floating-point coprocessor and 19% for the memory management and bus control. This left about 33% to be used for a data cache and an instruction cache. There are about 10 times as many transistors in the i860 as in the R2000—approximately 1 million—not 5 times as many as the above figures would imply. This is because much of the additional space is used for memory, and memory is very dense in transistors. Similiar figures could be quoted for the R4000.[7]

The development of these chips took longer than optimistic estimates had suggested, and in the meantime a surprisingly high performance was secured with off-chip caches, in particular by Hewlett-Packard and IBM.

In the long term, progress in VLSI is progress towards a larger scale of integration. However, in the short term, other considerations can have weight, as the above examples show. For example, it takes less time to design and test two simple chips than it does one more complex chip. Also, a set of two or three chips gives more product flexibility, since models in different price and performance ranges can be based on them. In the case of cache memory, advantage can be taken of the latest and highest performance commodity SRAM chips available at the time of going to market.

Sending Signals Across Chip Boundaries

If proper precautions are taken, it is possible to send signals from one chip to another at the speed of light which, allowing for the effect of dielectric material in the interconnect, is about 20 cm/nS. If this is achieved, the transit time between chips a few centimeters apart amounts only to a fraction of a nanosecond, which can be regarded as negligible at present clock speeds. It is necessary to use a transmission line of adequate quality—a good quality printed circuit board is sufficient for today's workstations—and to terminate it with its characteristic impedance. The transmission line presents a resistive impedance to the driving circuits at the sending end, and the speed at which signals can be sent is determined by the time taken to charge the pad and associated stray capacitances. What appears at the receiving end is a delayed, but otherwise close, copy of the waveform impressed on the sending end. The speed at which the pad can be charged is limited only by the amount of current the driver can supply.

The Cray 1 computer (first delivered in 1975) provides an illustration of what can be done if sufficient power is available. This computer used ECL transistors at a very low scale of integration and operated at high power. There were several hundred thousand chips mounted on more than 1,500 boards. Coaxial cable was used for interconnecting the boards. In spite of the very large number of inter-chip connections involved, the Cray 1 remained for a long time the fastest computer on the market, and its clock period of 12.5 nS is still respectable by modern standards. The price paid was a very high power consumption—about 100 kW.

On a modern high-density chip, the capacitance of a pad 100 microns square is somewhat less than 1 pF; the stray capacitance of the associated wiring is at least 2 pF and in addition the output transistor has an internal capacitance of, say, 2.5 pF. Since a matched transmission line presents a resistive impedance to the driving circuits, the interconnect wiring itself does not add to these capacitances.

The total capacitance is not large, and at current clock speeds there is no difficulty in designing drivers capable of charging it in much less than a clock cycle. However, the maximum

17 *The author, photographed in 1980 in the Computer Laboratory of Cambridge University, standing in front of a large disk, 31 inches in diameter, that was once one of a stack of 16 in a Data Products disk file used there from 1965 onwards. The disk file was 8 feet long, 3 feet wide, and stood about 6 feet high. There was one head assembly for each pair of surfaces and each assembly could be positioned independently. The total capacity was 40 Mbytes.*

Slightly to the left in the photograph is a disk taken from a disk cartridge similar to those shown in the photograph of the Xerox Alto in Figure 12 on page 36. Still further to the left is a floppy disk of the kind still used with many personal computers. At the bottom of the photograph, just to the left of the author, may be glimpsed the top of an interchangeable disk pack used in disk drives of the period around 1970, and since made obsolete by the modern hard disk.

rate of rise of an edge is one of the parameters of the design of a complex chip. If the design rate is exceeded, there will be trouble with noise spread throughout the chip via the power distribution wiring. Within current practice, charging the pad in half a clock cycle is reasonable, but to go much faster would be difficult.

If the basic RISC machine, the memory management unit, the TLB, and the cache control circuits are on different chips, repeated crossing of chip boundaries is a source of serious delay; this is why I said above that being able to put all these circuits on the same chip was an important landmark. However, there are situations in which pipelining comes to the designer's aid and enables the delay to be absorbed. An example is cache access. If, as is normally the case, the pipeline timing allows an address to be transmitted to an off-chip cache in the pipeline stage before that in which the word will be required, the delay can be accommodated. This is the reason why designs with off-chip caches have been competitive in the recent past.

As CMOS chips get larger, denser, and faster, inter-chip interconnect problems will get worse; for example, special steps will be necessary to mitigate the effects of clock skew. Equally it will become more difficult to send signals at high speed from one side of a large chip to the other. Eventually, as on-chip interconnecting wires become thinner and thinner, their resistance may become important, making it necessary to insert booster amplifiers in the middle of a long connection.

IBM RS6000

The IBM RS6000 was an outcome of work on the 801 minicomputer that had been in progress for some time in IBM research before RISC ideas came to be publicly discussed. The leader of the project was Dr. John Cocke. The RS6000 is composed of four chips with additional chips for the data cache. The total transistor count for the four chips is nearly 2 million, many more than it would have been possible to accommodate on a single chip at the time the design was worked out. One of the chips contains an integer RISC pipeline together with the control for the data cache. The pipelined floating-point unit has a chip to itself and comprises over 400,000 transistors. It was noticeably faster than other floating-point units designed at the same time. There is a separate chip for memory and I/O interface controls.

An especially interesting feature of the RS6000 is that branch instructions are executed in a branch processing unit and do not enter the main pipeline. The branch processing unit is accommodated on a chip which also contains the instruction dispatch unit and the instruction cache. In order to obtain maximum advantage from this arrangement, it is necessary for the memory to have sufficient bandwidth to allow both the target instruction and the follow-on instruction of a branch to be prefetched. Only one of these instructions is used and the extra work involved in fetching both of them represents the price that must be paid to ensure a smooth flow of instructions through the pipeline. Very similar techniques for processing branch instructions have long been used in large mainframes. In addition, the memory bandwidth in the RS6000 was sufficient to permit the dispatching, in the same clock cycle, of an integer instruction, a floating-point instruction, and an instruction for performing a Boolean operation on the contents of the condition register.

Memory Bandwidth

In the RS6000, the necessary memory bandwidth is obtained by providing four independently accessible memory modules with interleaved addressing. How to increase the memory bandwidth to keep up with the increasing speed of processor circuits is likely to be the main problem facing the designer of high-performance computers from now on.

To be effective, interleaving requires that there shall be at least four independent memory stacks. As we pass to higher capacity chips, this implies that the total memory capacity must be great. For example if 4-Mbit chips are used, the minimum memory will have a capacity of 64 Mbytes, since a single stack by itself provides a capacity of 16 Mbytes in 32-bit words. This may not matter at the high end, since much larger memories than this are in any case required. The development of chips with a smaller capacity but higher speed would be an obvious way to go, and this may happen. We are also likely to see schemes in which full advantage is taken of the ability of modern chips to hold a long word of bits in an internal buffer for repeated access. In this connection, it is worth remarking that a 16-Mbyte memory composed of 1-Mbyte chips is capable of reading 16 Kbytes into its internal registers in a single memory access cycle. A smart architect and a smart compiler ought to be able to make something of this.

Conventional data caches support data locality in one dimension only. For example, if a matrix is stored by rows, then elements in the same row or in adjacent rows may find their way into the cache, but elements that are in adjacent columns will not do so. In high-energy physics and many other subjects a numerical algorithm is as likely to require data words separated by a largish increment in the address space (referred to as a *stride*) as to require data words close together in the address space. Innovators are beginning to turn their thoughts to new forms of cache (if that word can properly be used to describe them) which support locality in terms of strides of any length from 1 upwards. Any solution to this problem is likely to come from the collaboration of computer architects, compiler writers, and operating system specialists.

Branch Prediction and Speculative Execution

The number of transistors that can be accommodated on a chip continues to quadruple every two years, and shortage of chip space is no longer the limiting factor that it was in 1992. For example, the DEC ALPHA chip, AXP 21164, described at Hot Chips V held in August 1994, contains nearly 9.6 million transistors. It is implemented with a feature size of 0.5 microns and the chip has an area of 3.0 square centimeters. Now that more space is available, it is possible to introduce into single chip computers more and more of the techniques that were pioneered in large mainframes, in particular in the IBM System 370 Model 91.

The DEC AXP 21164 illustrates the current move to achieve increased instruction level parallelism by designing the processor so that more than one instruction can be issued in the same clock cycle. The term *superscalar* is applied to processors of this kind. The AXP 21164 has four pipelines, two for integer operations and two for floating-point operations; in favorable circumstances, it is possible for an instruction to enter each of them in the same clock cycle.

The best way to secure high operating speed is by achieving a high clock rate. Unfortunately, the circuits needed for superscalar operation are complicated and there is a fundamental conflict involved in designing circuits that are both complicated and fast. The objects of superscalar operation would be defeated if it caused appreciable slowing of the clock. Every bit of skill the designer possesses must be exerted to avoid this happening.

So far superscalar processors preserve the order of operation of instructions specified in the program. The next generation will provide for out of order execution in cases where this will enable the rate of issue of instructions to be increased.

Branch prediction has received much attention in the literature in recent years, and many schemes for doing it at compile time have been investigated. Sufficient space is now available on processor chips for dynamic run-time prediction to be implemented. The principle is to record, in a specialized form of cache, the way branches go during the running of the program. It is then possible to make a prediction, based on this past experience, of the direction that future branches will take. I have heard it claimed that a hit rate of 95% can be achieved.

Along with branch prediction goes *speculative execution*, that is, allowing the processor to continue executing instructions in the direction of the predicted branch, before the outcome of the branch is known. It is necessary to retain sufficient information to enable the program to be restarted at the branch if the prediction proves to be false. An elegant scheme for doing this as far as the registers are concerned is known as *register renaming*. The idea is to make the register file contain more registers than are specified in the architecture. A subset of these are dynamically *named* as architectural registers and used by the pipeline as such. After a branch has occurred, *renaming* takes place in such a way that new registers take on the identity of those architectural registers that are in active use. If the branch prediction proves to have been correct, these registers are confirmed in their new identity; otherwise, the branch instruction is repeated using the old scheme of register naming.

Dual Processors

The use of more than one processor in a workstation naturally suggests itself as a way of gaining additional throughput. Two processors, symmetrically connected, would enable operating system processes to run in parallel with user processes and the workstation user would experience an enhanced responsiveness. There is currently some interest in this approach. Processor chips are becoming available which contain all the circuits necessary for cache coherence, so that they can be used in a dual processor configuration as they stand, without the need for additional "glue" chips.

With two processors, no special attention to programming would be necessary. A workstation with more than two processors would require specially optimized programs for its full exploitation, and would be of little advantage to the ordinary workstation user. Symmetric multiprocessor systems with more than two processors are, however, of interest in other contexts and are discussed in Essay Eight.

Continued Use of Mainframes

Applications suitable for workstations are steadily being moved off mainframes. However, not all applications are suitable—or the users concerned do not think they are suitable. In consequence, mainframes have continued to be bought, although in much smaller numbers than formerly. Some very large applications, for example certain database applications, are in principle capable of running on a non-personal workstation, but will continue to run on mainframes until such time as non-personal workstations of sufficient power are available.

Of a somewhat different nature are high-performance applications in scientific computing, especially in high-energy physics, computational chemistry, and so on. Here the requirement is for very high arithmetic performance, along with very wide memory bandwidth and very wide I/O bandwidth. At the extreme end are supercomputers—I use that term in the sense of the Cray 1 and its successors—which excel in the matter of bandwidth and are ideal for processing experimental data on a very large scale. These computers thus have a dual capability—very high speed for both fixed and floating-point operations and the capability of manipulating and processing very large volumes of data.

It may be expected that, before very long, workstations will be able to match the performance of the most powerful mainframes and supercomputers both as regards computing speed and as regards memory and I/O bandwidth. These workstations—"super non-personal workstations," as they may be called—will need memories that are very large and fast, disk arrays of immense capacity, and large bulk storage devices. This will put them in a price range very different from that of workstations as we now know them. They will also take up more space.

The Decline of ECL

At one time it seemed that ECL was firmly entrenched for the more powerful computers. It was intrinsically faster than CMOS and gained a factor of 6 in speed because it worked with a voltage swing of 0.6 instead of 3.5. This was possible because the crossover voltage for the switches was more sharply defined. The switching noise spread via the power supply was much less than with CMOS and the transistors were capable of switching larger powers. This gave an advantage in driving inter-chip connect. On the other hand, ECL, unlike CMOS, dissipates power when in a quiescent state as well as when switching, and the power consumption is in consequence much higher.

Beginning about 1990, there was a rapid growth of interest in BiCMOS, a process in which CMOS and ECL transistors can be formed on the same chip. This may have been in part due to the fact that BiCMOS also had potentiality for analog circuits. An early example of a processor implemented in BiCMOS was the Sun Super-SPARC.

The BiCMOS processes on which the above developments were based offered relatively poor ECL transistors; this was of no consequence, since CMOS transistors were used for storage and logic, while ECL transistors were used only for drivers. At the DEC Western Research Laboratory, a detailed design study was undertaken for an implementation based on a process—assuming one were available—that would yield ECL transistors of sufficiently good quality to enable them to be used for both logic and registers, with CMOS being used for current sources and for cache memory. The results of the design study were positive, but it was decided not to proceed to fabrication since no process of adequate performance was available at the time.

Earlier, Jouppi, Boyle, Dion et al. of DEC Western Research Laboratory had reported on an experimental program in which they designed and fabricated a major subset of the R3000 architecture in 1-micron ECL technology. They found that, while a single ECL gate occupies much more space than a CMOS gate, the disadvantage is reduced in practice since much more complex switching functions can be implemented in the same circuit. Enough partially working chips were obtained to show that such a processor could run at 300 Mhz with a power dissipation of 150 W.

There are indications that the advantages of ECL become less marked as feature sizes smaller than 0.5 micron are reached and may disappear altogether at very small feature sizes. It is hard to avoid the conclusion that the present outlook for both ECL and BiCMOS is distinctly unfavorable. This is very remarkable in view of the fact that ECL has been for so long the dominating technology for higher performance computers.

It has for some time been recognized that the CMOS process itself will begin to run into difficulties as feature sizes of less than one tenth of a micron are reached. Since the feature size of advanced CMOS chips has been halving every two years, it is not unreasonable to expect that this point will be reached around the end of this century. It is possible that the difficulties will be overcome, and that CMOS progress will continue well into the next century. However, eventually further shrinkage must either become impracticable or give no significant improvement in speed. It is impossible to predict what will then happen. Semiconductor engineers may come up with an improved bipolar process, or with some new form of process altogether. There may also be an opportunity for other semiconducting materials, such as gallium arsenide, to come into their own. No one can say what is likely to happen.

References

Grohoski, G.F. "Machine Organization of the IBM RISC System/6000 Processor." *IBM J. Res. & Dev.*, vol. 34, no. 1 (1990), p. 37.

IBM. *IBM RISC System/6000 Technology*. Publication No. SA23-2619, 1990.

Jouppi, N.P. et al. "A 300 Mhz 115W 32b ECL Microprocessor with On-chip Caches." *Proc. IEEE International Solid-State Circuits Conference*, 1993, p. 84.

ESSAY SEVEN

It's All Software Now!

A number of years ago I visited a young and successful computer company and was shown round by one of the directors. We passed offices in which people were working at computer terminals and I was told that they constituted the accounts department. A little further on we came to the software department, where there were also people using terminals. "Now," said my host, "I will show you the hardware department." Here, to my surprise, instead of the oscilloscopes and waveform analyzers that I was expecting, I saw more computer terminals. This was a sign of the times.

Printed Circuit Boards

Today, the designer of printed circuit boards, such as those intended to be plugged into a PC, has a great variety of software tools available to him. These include programs for layout and routing, and programs for checking that the design rules have been correctly followed. There are logic simulators for checking that the design is functionally correct, and more elaborate simulators for checking the timing. These tools make it possible to produce a working prototype without doing any experimental work on a laboratory bench.

In the dark ages of electronics, the debugging of circuits was carried out using experimental versions made by screwing the components down to a piece of wood and connecting them up. The behavior of the circuit was checked using an oscilloscope. These experimental versions were known as breadboards, because someone had compared them to boards on which bread was sliced. The wooden board went out long ago, but the term has survived. A modern version of the breadboard is the wire-wrapped prototype and this is still sometimes used. It is, however, costly in time and money and the effort spent on it does not advance the physical design of the final printed circuit board. Moreover, in certain respects, particularly as regards electrical interference and cross talk, the wire-wrapped version may give misleading information.

Design Rules for Silicon

Software tools are also available for the design of special chips, usually of the gate array variety, required for printed circuit boards. The electrical data for the transistors and on-chip interconnect, together with design rules to be followed, are supplied by the silicon foundry which will be responsible for the fabrication. If the designer keeps to the rules, then he can operate in a purely digital world and forget that in reality the transistors are analog devices whose behavior is only to be properly understood by those with a knowledge of semiconductor physics. Present-day chip designers need no more than a smattering of such knowledge.

The establishment of the above interface between the world of semiconductor physics and the world of digital circuit design is one of the striking achievements of the last fifteen years. It has established a framework in which the semiconductor industry and the computer industry can coexist and cooperate. An early landmark in this development was the publication in 1980 of a book entitled *Introduction to VLSI Systems* by Carver Mead and Lynn Conway. The interface is now well established and robust, but, as with other interfaces, those people who feel comfortable on both sides enjoy a certain advantage, particularly in knowing how far it is safe to bend the design rules at critical points.

Memory chips are a special case. The current high packing densities can only be obtained by thoroughly understanding and exploiting the analog properties of the elements of which they are composed. This must be done in terms of the particular semiconductor process line in use and in consequence memory chips are designed entirely within the semiconductor companies.

High Performance Processors

The fast single-chip processors that are now being designed contain a million or more transistors. At the high speed at which these transistors operate, the time taken for signals to pass from one transistor to another is a major factor in determining the maximum speed at which the chip can operate. The performance, therefore, depends on the physical construction and layout as much as on the switching time of the transistors. A breadboard would not only be very costly, but it would give no information about the performance to be expected.

For the reasons just mentioned, processor chips and other chips of similar complexity are now designed entirely within a computer using software tools. Functional simulators are available which take account of the switching times of the transistors and also of the time taken for signals to be propagated through the interconnect. It is possible, therefore, not only to check the correctness of the logic, but also to form a reliable estimate of the operating speed of the final chip. The design can be iterated until the designer is satisfied with the speed achieved. The first silicon is expected to work and usually it does, except perhaps for minor problems.

Simulators at the architectural level are useful for optimizing parameters such as cache configurations and sizes. To get representative results it is necessary to simulate a wide variety of real programs. The amount of computer time required to simulate an entire complex chip at the gate level is too great to permit the running of more than short, hand-coded assembly-language programs. Use is therefore made of mixed-mode simulators in which whole sections that have already been checked out—or have not yet been designed—can be modelled by a program. The speed at which the simulation can run is determined by the speed of the workstation or mainframe used. The time taken to design a chip can be reduced by running a variety of independent simulations simultaneously on a group of workstations. The problem of programming the workstations so that they can cooperate on a *single* simulation remains as a challenge to enthusiasts for parallel programming.

The purpose of a simulator is to enable a comprehensive series of tests to be applied to the processor under design. Devising these tests and interpreting the results is something that must be done by the design engineer himself with very little help from software. This part of the work makes great demands on the skill and engineering knowledge of the design team.

The effect of the developments here discussed has been to change the designer's way of working and the nature of the skills he needs, while leaving the intellectual and creative aspects of his task in essence unchanged. Formerly, a circuit designer needed, when checking out his design, the practical skills associated with working at a laboratory bench. Now, certain software skills are needed instead. The designer needs to be comfortable working with large software systems, and must know how to fight the system when that is necessary. Whether he or she needs to be an experienced software engineer is a matter for debate. If the designer works as a consultant or in a small company, it probably is necessary. In a large organization, a few software engineers can perhaps support a team of designers. It seems likely that, in the future, all circuit designers will have a strong software background.

Tools or Scaffolding?

Hammers and saws are tools that can be taken for granted. Everybody knows what their capabilities are as well as their limitations. The user can have confidence that, if properly used, they will not break. Few software tools are as robust as a hammer or a saw, or even an electric drill. Nevertheless, the metaphor is an appropriate one when the software is well tested and used in a familiar and well-mapped area. However, if the designer is working at the cutting edge of progress—for example, on the design of a new and very high performance processor—

he may well find that existing software is not good enough. He must be prepared to improve it or write his own new software. In these circumstances, I prefer to take an image from the building industry and to speak of scaffolding instead of tools. When a building is going up, the scaffolding is erected along with it by the same work force. It is designed to do its job and no more; if it proves inadequate in some respects, a fix can be improvised. When the building is complete the scaffolding is removed. It is not thrown away, but is retained in the hope that parts of it may prove serviceable for the next building.

For an advanced project there are many advantages in developing your own software in this way. Proprietary design software available on the market inevitably reflects the requirements and state of knowledge that existed at the time, perhaps several years in the past, when it was designed. Moreover, it will suffer from compromises designed to make it as widely applicable as possible. Software designed for a specific project can be simpler and more efficient than software designed to appeal to a wide market.

It is much in the interest of the project manager to have the design software completely under his own control. If he buys it from an independent supplier and does not have access to the source code, he will be in an especially difficult position, since he will have to rely on the vendor—whose priorities he does not control—for necessary enhancements and for the removal of bugs.

We are very far from having reached finality in our understanding of simulators and other items of design software. It is through the efforts of teams working at the limit of current technology and facing new challenges that the subject advances.

The Place of Formal Theory

For many years people with a theoretical turn of mind have been working towards the construction of proofs concerning the properties of programs, and more recently they have turned their attention to hardware. They aim, among other things, at being able to show that a processor design is consistent with a specification written in declarative form. The difficulties that stand in the way of developing this approach to the point at which it could replace simulation as a method for verifying the logic are great. Nevertheless, the effect has already been to bring theoreticians closer to the engineering world, and spin-off from their work into the main stream of design methodology is to be expected.

There have been attempts to capitalize on the magic word "proof" and to assert that a processor whose design has been "proved to be correct" will be safer in critical situations than one that has been developed in the usual way. It is true that the more checks that can be made, the less likely the design will be to contain bugs. It is an error, however, to suggest that "proving" has an absolute quality that puts it on an altogether different level than other methods of checking. For one thing, it is obvious that there is plenty of room for human error in drawing up the specification. A more fundamental objection is that the proof is necessarily performed in the digital domain, and has no relevance to an actual chip unless all the circuits on that chip do, in fact, behave in a digital manner. Should an error in the application of the design rules—or an error in the design rules themselves—cause a particular circuit sometimes to behave in an analog manner, the processor will make errors in spite of the proof.

CAD/CAM

The movement towards the use of a computer terminal and software tools for design is not confined to the computer industry. For example, there are mechanical CAD / CAM systems which enable an engineer working at a terminal to design a component intended to be manufactured on a numerically controlled machine tool. The system generates instructions for the machine tool that correspond exactly to the data for making masks that are sent to a silicon foundry. The designer is provided with various aids for verifying that the design meets its specification. He or she can view graphical representations of the component from various angles and can examine its behavior under stress, making use, for example, of a finite-element package. Again, some of the manufacturing rules to which a designer must work are codified and automatically applied, unless he chooses to override them. In particular, the system will specify the appropriate type of cutter to be mounted on the machine tool and the appropriate rate of cut. The CAD/CAM system replaces the drawing board and the slide rule in the same way that design automation in the computer industry has replaced the breadboard and the oscilloscope.

References

Mead, C.A and L.A. Conway. *Introduction to VLSI Systems*. Reading, Mass.: Addison-Wesley, 1980.

ESSAY EIGHT

The Lure of Parallelism and Its Problems

Massively parallel computing systems have appealed and continue to appeal to many people, and they appeal for a variety of different reasons. Some take the view that the stored program computer—the Eckert–von Neumann computer—is not necessarily the last word and that some other model or paradigm in which parallelism plays a major role might come to supersede it. They see, dimly over the horizon, a new world of rewarding endeavor and experience in which computer design will take on a new dimension and in which levels of performance at present undreamt of will be achieved. That is what I refer to as the lure of parallelism.

For others, the importance of parallelism is that it provides an avenue—the only avenue—by which it will be possible to go on achieving higher performance when the limit of speed for a uniprocessor is reached. The urgency they attach to work on parallelism depends on the imminence with which they perceive that stage being reached.

Very early in the history of computer development, people remarked that the speed of light sets a limit to the speed with which signals can be sent from one part of a computer to another and hence to the speed at which computers of a given physical size can operate.

In fact, signals pass from one part of a silicon chip to another along wires loaded with capacitance. It is the time taken to charge this capacitance that determines the speed of operation, rather than the time taken for electromagnetic waves to travel the relevant distance. Present processors are consequently much smaller than they would have to be if signals traveled across the chip with the velocity of light. However, the conclusion remains the same: in order to get faster, computers must get smaller.

At various times in the past there have been false alarms when it has appeared to many observers that there was danger of progress in high-speed processor development slowing down and coming to a halt. Always the innovative powers of semiconductor engineers have been equal to the challenge and the alarms have proved abortive. Now we have a new alarm and this time it is one that we should certainly take seriously. It is more than likely that around the end of the decade it will be possible to make semiconductor circuits with feature sizes of 0.1 micron. At around this point further speeding up of CMOS, as we know it, may well become impossible. ECL already seems to have dropped out of the race. There is thus a real possibility that progress will come to an end. However, one does not have to be a very great optimist to believe that CMOS has more life in it than the above estimate suggests or that the exploitation of new materials and/or new phenomena will enable progress to be carried at least one stage further.

When electronic systems reach their eventual limit, there remains the theoretical possibility that purely optical systems will come in. As I pointed out above, present day processors are much smaller than they would need to be if the velocity of light were the limiting factor. Without going to a higher degree of miniaturization, therefore, a purely optical system could in theory carry us on for at least another order of magnitude in speed. It is important to add that at present there is no sign of the major breakthrough that would be necessary. We would need some form of gating system in which one light beam could control the passage of another light beam without any electronic circuits being involved. Current developments in optoelectronics, using, for example, gallium arsenide, interesting as they are in their own sphere, do not hold out the possibility of this breakthrough, since the speed at which they operate is determined by the electronics rather than by the optics.

Multiprocessors and Multicomputers

The term *multiprocessor* refers to a system in which a number of processors work out of the same memory. A *multicomputer* consists of separate computers, each with its own memory, communication between them taking place by messages passing along fixed links. Intermediate between multiprocessors and multicomputers are systems in which the processors have both private memory and access to shared memory.

A well-known example of a multicomputer is the Hypercube, in which the processors are thought of as being located at the corners of an *n*-dimensional cube; each processor has hardware links to the *n* processors at the adjacent corners. The programmer is responsible for organizing the explicit sending and receiving of messages.

A multiprocessor, with a number of identical processors and a number of memory modules interconnected via a bus, is known as a symmetric multiprocessor. It can be regarded as a direct descendant of the dual processors that began to appear as an option in mainframes in the late 1960s. These had special circuits designed to keep their two caches coherent. A significant breakthrough took place in the early 1980s when the principle of the snoopy cache was evolved.[8] This was not limited to two processors, but could be applied to any number, with the amount of equipment required being proportional, or nearly so, to the number of processors. Typically, there is enough memory bandwidth to support sixteen, or even more, processors.

Symmetric multiprocessors of minicomputer performance enjoyed a certain success in the 1980s, although they did not come to dominate the market as some enthusiasts thought they would. They were not intended to be competitive with supercomputers for single, highly optimized jobs. They were at their best when providing a time-sharing system with a mixed load of jobs, some requiring a single processor only and some capable of using more. With a favorable mix of jobs all the processors could be kept busy most of the time. In this way, high throughput, together with some speeding up of the parallel jobs, could be achieved.

Currently, there is interest in symmetric multiprocessors in which the individual processors are of supercomputer performance. These are seen in the supercomputer world as providing scope for gaining speed by parallelism, while keeping within the mainstream of computer development. At Hot Chips III, a symposium held in August 1991 and devoted to leading-edge chips of various kinds, a term much used by presenters of advanced RISC processor chips was *multiprocessor ready*, meaning that the design of the on-chip cache, its communications with the outside world, and the bus interface all took account of the requirements of a symmetric multiprocessor architecture. The ultimate limit to this form of architecture is set by the traffic-carrying capacity of a bus.

Until recently, there were few constraints on what might plausibly be proposed for a highly parallel architecture. The result was that many different ones were proposed; each had its own programming framework and set of tricks, and there was a danger that the consequent fragmentation of effort might retard the progress of parallel processing. Now that very powerful single-chip processors have come to dominate the computer architecture scene, those parallel architectures which can use such chips as building blocks have a head start over architectures which cannot reach their potential without the development of special (high-density) chips. We may therefore expect to see the more exotic architectures drop out.

An example of an architecture which has long had its advocates but which, for the above reason among others, is unlikely to be much heard of in the future, is the single instruction multiple data (SIMD) architecture. ILLIAC 4, designed in the late 1960s, was a pioneer of this approach. SIMD machines consist of an array of computers, each computer being connected to its neighbors in both the X and Y directions. The single instruction stream is decoded by a central processor. The central processor executes branch instructions itself and broadcasts the others to the array.

It has now become possible to put a significant number of powerful processors on one chip. However, there is as yet no sign of the development of a system philosophy on which such an approach could be effectively based.

Data Flow

Data flow stands apart as being the most radical of all approaches to parallelism and the one which has been the least successful. Data flow machines are defined in the *Encyclopedia of Computer Science*, edited by Anthony Ralston and Edwin Reilly, as machines whose actions are determined by the availability of the data needed for those actions. The basic principle is that, subject to the availability of a processing unit, instructions in the program are executed as soon as their operands become available. It is expected that normally there will be enough instructions ready to run for all or most of the processing units to be kept busy.

These ideas are both simple and elegant. However, deep problems, connected with the addressing of memory and the execution of loops, are encountered when any attempt is made to base a practical machine on them. In consequence, no consensus has been reached as to what the architecture of a data flow machine should be, nor has anything been built that in any way matches conventional computers. The present outlook for data flow is far from good. If any practical machine based on data flow ideas and offering real power ever emerges, it will be very different from what the originators of the concept had in mind.

Achieving Speed by Parallelism

It cannot be too strongly stressed that the central problem in developing a fast program to run in parallel on a number of processors is to spread the load between the processors, so that there is very little idle time. You do not achieve high speed by having idle processors.

It follows that it is not enough to be able to identify threads in the program that can run in parallel on separate processors and eventually join up. If one of the threads runs for say, 1 second, before halting, while all the others run for less than 0.1 second, most of the processors will be idle for most of the time. The resulting gain in speed will consequently be minimal.

Unfortunately, it is usually impracticable to figure out the time required for a thread to complete by staring at the static code or by analyzing it with a computer program. Indeed, in the general case it is impossible. The programmer must therefore proceed by trial and error, running the program, measuring the processor idle time, and then seeing what can be done to improve the situation.

One of the attractions of data flow when it was originally proposed was that it offered parallelism at the level of individual instructions, so that spreading the load between processing units would have been automatic.

Not a Matter of Repeating a Success

There are some who have noted the development of optimizing compilers for uniprocessors, and taking this as a precedent have thought that it will be only a matter of time before compiler specialists learn how to do the same for parallel computing. People who take this view have not, in my opinion, sufficiently appreciated the very different nature of the two situations.

No one has ever suggested that the use of high-level languages with optimizing compilers could be a way of writing programs that would run faster than programs optimized by hand. What high-level languages give is vastly increased programmer productivity and they do this at the expense of performance. With a good optimizing compiler, the loss of performance is not substantial, but even if it were programmers would still choose high-level languages.

In the writing of parallel programs the exact opposite is true. The attainment of a high running speed is the primary objective, at the cost if necessary—and it nearly always is necessary—of the programmer having to face much hard work by brain and hand.

A compiler for a conventional high-level language can do such things as eliminating the redundant evaluation of common subexpressions, removing statements from loops, and, perhaps, replacing tail recursion by iteration. That is to say, it acts at a rather mechanical level. If the programmer has structured his program badly, or chosen a poor algorithm, the compiler cannot help him.

The work of writing and optimizing a parallel program is far from mechanical. It involves the design of an effective parallel algorithm, or the rearrangement of an existing algorithm, and implementing it in such a way that the processors are as fully loaded as possible. As I have pointed out above, trial and error will normally be necessary. Success can depend critically on how effectively data and code are allocated to appropriate memories or memory modules. If success is elusive, there is nothing for it but to start again with a new or revised algorithm.

In the present state of knowledge, all of the above needs human effort, and the chances of ever being able to automate it significantly are, in my view, negligible. It is a pipe dream to hope that it will become possible to write a compiler that will take a program written in C (for example) and automatically optimize it to run efficiently on arbitrary parallel hardware.

It is sometimes suggested that there would be merit in using a non-procedural or declarative language, leaving the choice of algorithm to the compiler. I find this approach interesting, but nothing I have seen so far leads me to think that it offers great hope.

When the Development of Parallel Programs Is Worthwhile

If the human effort required to develop a good parallel program—and the machine time consumed—is to be justified, two conditions must be satisfied: (1) speed must be of first importance and (2) the resulting program must have a long useful life. Added to this there must be a clear understanding that when new hardware is shipped in, or when existing hardware is upgraded to a significant extent, the work will as likely as not have to be done over again.

These conditions were first found to be satisfied in high-energy physics, and there was much success with optimizing programs for the Cray 1 and its vector hardware. Now parallel computers of various kinds are coming into use, and more and more areas are emerging in which people are willing to devote time and effort to optimizing programs for them.

This activity is all taking place at the top end of the computer range. This is because the investment in human effort necessary to develop a program for a parallel computer is so great that no one would make it if the same result could be achieved by using a uniprocessor based on faster technology.

The key people in parallel computing are those who know the scientific field concerned and the algorithms appropriate to it. Progress may involve mathematical research and fresh insights into the best way to model the physical situation and what approximations to make. The pure computer specialist can help by providing a good programming environment, languages with good facilities for handling threads, and tools for making the performance measurements mentioned above. However, important as these are, they go only a small part of the way.

Certain areas lend themselves especially well to parallelism. One such area is signal processing where large factors of improvement over a conventional uniprocessor may be obtained, particularly if specially built equipment is used. If, however, we confine ourselves to the type of computing that can be regarded as the natural development of general-purpose computing as we now know it, and consider the speedup of the entire program, not merely of the parts that can be parallelized, we find that very modest speedup factors are often all that can be obtained. However, on specially favorable problems, a speedup factor approaching the number of processors in use may be obtained. Exactly what may be achievable in the foreseeable future is a controversial topic. At present, it is often a struggle to achieve a factor of more than a small integer. The speedup factor attained is not to be assessed simply by measuring the amount of idle time with the particular algorithm in use. An alternative algorithm may be faster, even if there is more idle time.

The Importance of Fast Serial Performance

It typically happens that while some parts of a program can be speeded up by parallelization, other parts are inherently serial. In such cases the aim should be to optimize the parallel parts until the computation time is dominated by the serial parts, since, even if it were possible to go further, the increase of speed obtained would be marginal. However, if it were possible to make the serial hardware faster, there would be a proportional decrease in the running time of the problem.

Thus it can easily happen that the ultimate running speed on a problem that lends itself to parallelization is determined by the speed with which the hardware can run a serial problem. For this reason, if a parallel computer is to get full advantage from parallel hardware it must have the highest possible serial performance. This fact was thoroughly appreciated by the designers of the Cray 1 which, in addition to offering parallelism in the form of vector operations, had faster serial operations than any other computer of its day. If the designers of new processor chips, in their anxiety to make them multiprocessor ready, accept any significant reduction in serial speed, they are likely to be disappointed when it comes to ultimate performance.

Outlook

We have now reached the point at which designers of supercomputers intended for numerical computation take it for granted that they should offer multiprocessor or multicomputer configurations. This coincides with a major expansion of the role of numerical calculation in physics, engineering, and other subjects, as simulations based on physical laws or on stochastic models find wider use. In each field, a limit to progress is set by the number of people who can be assembled to develop the parallel programs.

There is as yet insufficient experience of parallel computing to be able to say to what extent experience obtained in one application field can, to a useful degree, be transferred to another. One would expect that purely programming advances would be transferable, but that progress in problem formulation and the development of algorithms would be more field-specific.

As between the fields, I would expect progress to be uneven, many proving resistant to the application of parallel computation, but some showing spectacular results. It is my personal view that modest factors of speedup compared with the best uniprocessor programs are likely to be the rule rather than the exception.

References

Goodman, J.R. "Using Cache Memory to Reduce Processor Memory Traffic." *Proc. 10th Annual Int. Symp. on Computer Architecture*, 1983, pp. 124–31.

PART THREE

Software

ESSAY NINE

Software and the Programmer

Engineering could not exist without mathematics and experimental science. Mathematics deals in pure thought and experimental science is concerned with the laws of nature. Within the same framework, it may be said that the aim of engineering is to secure control over nature. In some branches of engineering the dependence is very clear. Where, for example, would heat engines be without thermodynamics, radio antenna design without electromagnetic theory, or communications without Fourier analysis? It has long been accepted that the training of an engineer should include a serious study of mathematics and the relevant science, whatever use he may subsequently make of what he learns.

Software is a new subject and it is not clear how it should be regarded. If control over computers is control over nature, then software is a form of engineering. It is an unusual form, however, in that, while software is a practical subject, it has no direct connection with experimental science as that term is ordinarily understood. A piece of software can be as complex as a segment of DNA, but its complexity is not the complexity of nature; it is the product of the human brain.

Some people have seen a close connection between software and mathematics. Donald Knuth includes a lot of mathematics in his book *The Art of Computer Programming*, but not all of this helps the reader understand the programming methods he describes. In particular, many of the exercises set for the reader are mathematical problems suggested by those methods, for example, to enumerate the trees of a certain type. These problems interested Knuth and he no doubt thought that he could make his treatment more interesting to his readers by including them. This may be true for mathematically minded students, but I would have thought that the average student would find running programming exercises on a computer more interesting than solving mathematical problems. The mathematics does, however, give an intellectual stiffening to the subject and I shall return later to the need for this.

Programmers and Software Engineers

A modern programmer, or software engineer, makes use of a workstation which provides powerful desktop computing facilities; it also gives access, via a local area network, to extensive remote filing and other services. A programmer depends on a team to support the system he or she uses, but the actual work is done entirely with his or her own hand and brain. The development of modern workstations and programming environments has made it possible for immense power to be put at the disposal of one person. If that person is a programmer, he or she can handle every stage of a large programming project—taking a broad view of the work, as well as working on details when necessary. The result is to make the modern programmer an autonomous professional with full responsibility for the work done.

This present status of programmers contrasts with an earlier one, when attempts were made to treat them as low-level technicians who worked with other programmers in a team. The systems analyst in charge was supposed to allocate the work of each member of the team in detail and to lay down the interfaces between them. This was many years ago when the difficulties of managing software projects had first begun to give rise to concern, and it was thought that the solution might be to manage software projects in the same way that hardware projects were managed. The programmer, or coder as he or she was then often called, was thought of in the same light as a technician working at a bench. However, there were other people who had a more exalted idea of the professional status that should be accorded to programming. In the period before time-sharing had become accepted, Harlan Mills did something to make that idea a reality with his concept of a *chief programmer team*.

The term "software engineer" is highly appropriate within a company that designs products for the market, the design of products being a traditional function of an engineer. It is less appropriate in other cases. For example, it would not be appropriate in the case of a professional programmer who is a member of a physics research team and who is measured on the value of his or her work in relation to the research rather than for its marketability. However, from the point of view of their day-to-day work, all programmers who work on major projects have essentially the same task, whether they choose to call themselves software engineers or not.

Like other professionals, programmers have their individual tastes and adopt the methods of working they are most comfortable with. There are styles of programming and program development as there are styles of management. I reject the myth that there is a particular style or discipline of programming that is to be preferred above all others. In particular, I do not think that there is any specific style of programming that should be taught to software engineers.

Intellectual Stiffening

The training of software engineers—like that of other professionals who work with their hands and their brains—must have a large practical element. Professional training, however, needs intellectual stiffening as well. This presents no problem in professions based on an established academic subject, for example medicine or the law, nor does it present any problem in the older branches of engineering based on the physical sciences. It is far from clear, however, what software engineers or computer scientists should be taught that they will perceive as being relevant to their work. At one time hardware design would have been a natural choice, but that subject now divides sharply into architecture and semiconductor technology. Architecture has become too like software, with the physics all wrapped away behind design rules, to provide the stiffening required. On the other hand, it is hard to see how an in-depth study of semiconductor physics and process technology would be appropriate for a programmer.

Very often mathematics is used as a stiffener for a computer science course. As I have already indicated, I am not very happy with this approach. Many students who are attracted to a practical career find mathematics uncongenial and difficult; certainly it is not the most popular part of an engineering course for the majority of students. Admittedly, mathematics trains people to reason, but reasoning in real life is not of a mathematical kind. Physics is a far better training in this respect.

The truth may be that computer science does not by itself constitute a sufficiently broad education, and that it is better studied in combination with one of the physical sciences or with one of the older branches of engineering. I believe that I am not alone in thinking that, as an education, computer science by itself fails to bring out the best in people.

I would like to see computer science teaching set deliberately in an historical framework. For example, a course on operating systems should trace the evolution of operating systems from early batch monitors and time-sharing systems to the systems in current use. Selected systems that were important in their day and contributed to the progress of the subject should be examined in detail. Students need to understand how the present situation has come about, what was tried, what worked and what did not, and how improvements in hardware made progress possible. The absence of this element in their training causes people to approach every problem from first principles. They are apt to propose solutions that have in the past been found wanting. Instead of standing on the shoulders of their precursors, they try to go it alone.

Engineering Schools and Computer Studies

There is a tendency for new branches of engineering to have little connection at first with established engineering departments and professional institutes. It is some time before the new branches become recognized by the engineering establishment as being "proper" engineering. A good example is afforded by radio engineering. Most of the radio and electronic engineers of my generation had degrees in physics. Although they played a key role in the development of a new industry, for a long time they felt themselves to be outsiders in the electrical engineering profession.

I believe that, in the same way, computer science will come to be regarded as part and parcel of engineering and will be so recognized by the professional bodies. The core subjects—computer architecture, system software, and programming technology—will be taught in all major university engineering schools. This does not mean that some parts of computer science will not also be taught in mathematics departments, where the emphasis will be different.

In the past, new engineering disciplines have sometimes found their place as subdivisions of older ones. Others, for example chemical engineering, have become engineering disciplines in their own right. Computer science may go the same way. On the other hand, computer scientists, like control engineers, have a kindred feeling for electrical engineers, and may, perhaps, join up with them; indeed, "EE and CS" is already familiar in certain universities as the name for a department. We must wait to see whether things will go in this way or whether, within engineering schools, computer science will emerge as an engineering discipline in its own right.

References

Baker, F.T. "Chief Programmer Team Management of Structured Programming." *IBM Systems Journal*, vol. 11, no. 1 (1972), pp. 56–73.

Knuth, D.E. *The Art of Computer Programming,* vol. 2, 2nd ed. Reading, Mass.: Addison-Wesley, 1981.

ESSAY TEN

From FORTRAN and ALGOL to Object-Oriented Languages

In the latter part of 1952 and 1953, people began to experiment with symbolic programming systems and these can now be recognized as the remote ancestors of modern high-level programming languages. However, the first major landmarks in the development of programming languages were the announcement of FORTRAN in April 1957 and the issuing of the ALGOL 60 report in 1960.

The FORTRAN group worked within IBM and were in close touch with users of IBM 704 computers in industrial and university environments. Although they broke much new ground, both in language design and in compiler technology, they never lost sight of their main objective, namely, to produce a product that would be acceptable to practical users with real problems to solve. In this they were very successful. There was, of course, much skepticism, and it would be wrong to say that users of IBM 704s across the United States switched from assembly

18 *Adriaan van Wijngaarden joined the Mathematical Centre in Amsterdam in 1947. He was a prominent member of the ALGOL 60 group, and later became the designer of a successor language, ALGOL 68. One of his first assignments at the Mathematical Centre had been to establish a desk machine computing service and he is here seen with such a machine on his desk.*

(Courtesy of SMC/CWI, Amsterdam.)

language programming to FORTRAN overnight; however, many of those who were persuaded to give FORTRAN a try became enthusiastic.

ALGOL 60 was the work of an international group with members from Germany, Switzerland, the U.S., England, Denmark, etc. The spade work had been done as a result of an earlier initiative taken by a small group of mathematicians in Switzerland and Germany with a background in numerical analysis. ALGOL 58, as their language was called, was of short-lived importance. It did, however, provide a starting point for the ALGOL 60 group which met for one week of intensive activity in Paris in 1960. At the end of the week they were able to agree on a report that stood the test of time.

The ALGOL group, although international in composition, was dominated by its continental members. In 1960, there were very few powerful computers on the continent of Europe and these members, unlike their FORTRAN counterparts, were not used to struggling with the day-to-day problems of getting work through a computer center. Their interest was more theoretical. Their aim was to define a language based on coherent principles that would be as free as possible from *ad hoc* constructions. They were determined not to be influenced by implementation difficulties for any particular machine and, if a feature in the language made efficient implementation difficult, then so be it. Nevertheless, they had in mind a very clear implementation model, namely, that the language was to be implemented on a stack. All memory allocation was to take place on the stack. This model dominated the design of the language. The scope rules of ALGOL 60—by which a variable declared in a block could only be accessed in the block itself, or in blocks interior to it—naturally followed.

ALGOL 60 made little headway in the United States as a practical computing language, being taken up by only one major manufacturer, namely Burroughs. This was no doubt principally for the practical reasons I have mentioned. Another reason was that computer users generally were not prepared for the abstract sophistication of the ALGOL language. Most of them had been trained in other disciplines such as physics and engineering, rather than in pure mathematics. As far as computing went, they saw themselves as practical people solving real problems and felt a distrust for those whom they regarded as having their heads in the clouds. This attitude did not entirely disappear until the effect of computer science teaching in the universities made itself felt.

A particular feature which helped to distance practical people from the ALGOL enthusiasts was recursion. On the advocacy of John McCarthy, who had only a few years before developed the LISP language, the ALGOL group decided that all procedures should be recursive. This decision accorded well with their philosophy of implementation on a stack. The long-term rightness of this decision has become amply apparent, but at the time it was a concept that many people found difficult to understand; even when they had understood it, they could not see what good it was, and they feared that it might do harm by leading to inefficiency.

When a change was made to an ALGOL program, recompilation of the whole program was necessary. The same problem has continued to plague block-structured languages ever since. The need for continual recompilation was a serious disadvantage at a time when most computers made use of slow punched card readers for input.

In FORTRAN, which had no block structure—and may therefore be described as a *flat* language—separate compilation presented no difficulty. The FORTRAN Monitor System for batch processing came into use about 1958 and made it especially easy to combine, in the same program, parts written in FORTRAN with others written in assembly code. The FORTRAN Monitor System broke new ground, and may be regarded as the forerunner of modern operating systems. It was a major factor in promoting the general adoption of FORTRAN.

As time went on, ALGOL-type languages gradually became accepted for non-numerical programming, including system programming, and also to some extent for small- and medium-scale numerical programming. However, people engaged in large-scale numerical computation—especially in nuclear and atomic physics—remained loyal to FORTRAN. This was partly because their programs were relatively simple in logical structure, and FORTRAN provided all they needed. Moreover, users of the Cray 1 computer found that FORTRAN, with some special features added, enabled them to optimize their programs to take full advantage of vector hardware. FORTRAN, in the version known as FORTRAN 77, is still by far the most popular language for numerical computation, although C is making a small amount of progress, especially among the younger programmers.

Programming Languages as a Scientific Study

As a subject for study, ALGOL early attracted widespread interest in the universities in the United States as elsewhere. In fact, a major achievement of the ALGOL pioneers was to create a new academic discipline, namely, the scientific study of programming languages. This discipline had its practical side and its theoretical side. The theoreticians found challenging problems in syntax definition and syntax analysis; later, when the most important of these challenges had been successfully met, they moved to other computer-related areas, notably to complexity theory.

The block structure proved a fruitful idea; in particular, the use of a single stack provided a simple and automatic method of recycling memory that was no longer in use. However, it is unfortunate that block structure continued for so long to dominate, to the exclusion of all other models, the thoughts of academic language specialists. In particular, it is in my view regrettable that a scientific study of flat languages such as FORTRAN was not made, and their merits and potentialities evaluated in the light of what had been learned from ALGOL.

As long as the stack remained the kingpin on which all memory allocation depended, there was no hope of advances in modularity or data hiding. The first sign of a break away from pure block structure was the appearance in advanced languages of the heap. Allocation of memory from the heap was an alternative to allocating space on the top of the stack. This paved the way for object-oriented programming which is, in my view, the most important development in programming languages that has taken place for a long time.

Technicalities apart, an object-oriented language provides the programmer with two major benefits, namely, modularity and data hiding. A program is composed of a number of modules; each module is self-contained, has a clear interface to other modules, and is capable of being separately compiled. The writer of a module can decide for himself the extent to which the data within it are to be protected from misuse or accidental corruption by being hidden from the outside world.

The introduction of a heap required a new policy for recovering memory no longer in use. It was at first assumed that an automatic garbage collector along the lines of that used in LISP would be essential. It is true that list processing in the LISP sense would be very difficult without a garbage collector; however, experience has shown that for much work the programmer can get on quite well without one. For example, few implementations of C++ rejoice in a garbage collector. The programmer has to take care that leakage of memory does not become a problem.

The heap, with a garbage collector, and classes (a seminal concept on the way to object-oriented programming) were to be found in Simula 67. The importance of these features to programming language in general was only slowly realized. This was perhaps because Simula was offered to the world as a simulation language rather than as a general-purpose language.

Object-oriented programming languages may still be described as being in a state of evolution. No completely satisfactory language in this category is yet available. Modula-3 is well designed, but it has so far attracted attention mainly in research circles and as a language for teaching. C++ may fairly be described as an object-oriented language and can handle large problems, but it shows signs of its non–object-oriented origins.

Compatibility

Designers of programming languages—whether they are individuals or committees—differ in their attitude to compatibility. How easy should they make it to convert a program written in an old language to the new language?

Recently, a new ISO standard for FORTRAN has been adopted. This is known as FORTRAN 90 and its designers hope that it will eventually come into general use to replace

FORTRAN 77. The whole of FORTRAN 77 is included within FORTRAN 90 so that existing programs will run without change.

It is harder to imagine a stricter view of compatibility, but it at once creates a problem. Users who change over to FORTRAN 90 will presumably wish to make use of the new features, for otherwise they would have no motivation to make the change. They will have to adapt their style of programming, dropping FORTRAN 77 features that are regarded as outmoded and embracing the newer facilities. The FORTRAN 90 standard gives some indications as to what those features are, but most users will need formal training if they are to use the language to best advantage.

Niklaus Wirth took a less strict view of compatibility when he designed the well-known language Pascal. This is a close relation of ALGOL 60, and it is easy for an ALGOL 60 programmer to learn; however, there was never any thought that a Pascal compiler might be able to accept ALGOL 60 programs. Wirth has designed a number of languages. Each represents his developing view of what a language should be like. If you adopt one of Wirth's languages, then you must go along with his view of how computer programs should be written. He puts stress on elegance of structure, with few if any exceptions to the rules, and on the elimination of unnecessary or redundant features. His aim is to produce a "lean" language that can be described in a slim manual and is easy to learn.

C++ was designed by Bjarne Stroustrup who took as his starting point the language C. Stroustrup aimed at producing a language that was cleaner than C and one that would make object-oriented programming possible. He was not so much concerned with elegance in the mathematical sense. He was chary of tailoring the language to his own, possibly limited, view of what would be good for users. In fact, in order to make sure that he did not unintentionally create difficulties for people whose work was in programming areas which they understood better than he did, he retained various constructs from C that he did not particularly like.

Stroustrup remarked to me recently that "my impression is that most other language designers are less reluctant to impose their views on programmers and that some consider such imposition their duty." As a result, C++ does not impose any particular style of programming on the programmer. A designer who takes this view, however, has the duty to give advice to programmers on how to develop an appropriate style of programming, and Stroustrup thoroughly accepts this duty.

If I had to draw any conclusion from these observations on current developments, it would be that the subject of programming languages, in spite of its thirty-five years of existence, is still a very immature one. I do not believe that, to be suitable for very large problems as well as for small ones, a programming language has itself to be large and covered with warts. On the contrary, I believe that one day we will have simple and powerful languages that do not force unnatural ways of working on the programmer whatever his field. More experimentation is needed, but I am optimistic enough to hope that we are more than halfway to reaching that goal.

References

Backus, John. "The History of FORTRAN I, II and III." *History of Programming Languages*, ed. Richard L. Wexelblat. (Report of the ACM SIGPLAN Conference held January 1978.) New York: Academic Press, 1981, pp. 25–74.

Lee, J.A.N. and Henry Tropp, eds. "Twenty-fifth Anniversary of FORTRAN." *Ann. Hist. Comp.*, vol. 6, no. 1, special issue (1984).

Naur, Peter. "The European Side of the Last Phase of the Development of ALGOL." *History of Programming Languages*, ed. Richard L. Wexelblat. (Report of the ACM SIGPLAN Conference held January 1978.) New York: Academic Press, 1981, pp. 92–139.

Naur, P., ed. "Report on the Algorithmic Language ALGOL 60." *Comm. ACM*, vol. 3 (1960), pp. 299–314.

Perlis, Alan J. "The American Side of the Development of ALGOL." *History of Programming Languages*, ed. Richard L. Wexelblat. (Report of the ACM SIGPLAN Conference held January 1978.) New York: Academic Press, 1981, pp. 75–91.

Stroustrup, Bjorne. "A History of C++: 1979–1991." In Proc. 2nd ACM SIGPLAN History of Programming Languages Conference. *ACM SIGPLAN Notices*, vol. 28, no. 3 (1993), pp. 271–98.

Wirth, N. "Recollections About the Development of Pascal." In Proc. 2nd ACM SIGPLAN History of Programming Languages Conference. *ACM SIGPLAN Notices*, vol. 28, no. 3 (1993), pp. 333–42.

ESSAY ELEVEN

Operating Systems in a Changing World

The principles by which processes are queued and managed, laid down at the early Symposia on Operating System Principles (SOSP), still remain valid. Since then new insights have led to important advances. For example, insights into the user interface have led to the development of windows and menus. At a different level, authentication—the process by which the system can become sure that a person demanding resources is the person he or she claims to be—has become well understood. Authentication is the necessary basis on which resource allocation and billing, as well as security, can be based.

I shall begin by commenting on the past lessons that have been learned and on the experience that has been gained. I shall then go on to discuss present research directions.

Lessons Learned and Experience Gained

Process Management

Much early effort was devoted to understanding cooperating processes and the design of synchronization primitives. This was successful and the days are now long over when an operating system would stop every few hours, or every few days, because of some arcane synchronizing error that was hard to pinpoint. While there is always scope for research, synchronization is no longer a principal preoccupation of operating systems specialists.

In the 1960s and 1970s, a popular area of research was the analysis of operating systems in terms of queueing theory. Each resource—files, memory, processor, etc—had a queue associated with it. This was in days of limited I/O bandwidths and minimal resources generally, and it was natural to view the passage of tasks through an operating system as being like the movement of cars in Manhattan on a busy day, with queues at every intersection.

In my view, queueing theory failed to produce any results of particular value. This was partly because of its inadequacy as a mathematical discipline. In order to get results it was usually necessary to assume an exponential probability distribution; this was particularly unfortunate when analyzing a time-sharing system, since tasks generated by users tend to fall into two groups, short and long, giving rise to a bimodal distribution. Nowadays, we have more resources and more bandwidth and we like to think of tasks moving through a system like cars moving along a freeway.

An important development of recent years is the concept of threads. Threads are a development of the long-standing concept of lightweight processes, that is, processes which can be rapidly created and destroyed without the overheads associated with regular processes. Lightweight processes are important to system designers since they make it possible to use processes freely in the structuring of a system. Since threads run in the same address space as the process that spawns them, they can communicate with low overheads.

Interprocess communication may be effected in a time-sharing system either by passing messages or by making use of shared memory. Hugh Lauer and Roger Needham showed that the two methods are essentially equivalent, and that the choice between them is largely a matter of convenience. Message passing may also be used to provide communication between processes running in separate computers, for example, between a user process running in a workstation and one running in a file server. Appreciation of this fact led to vigorous discussion on the subject of remote procedure calls. This discussion—and a parallel discussion of other communication primitives—drew attention to the ease with which bandwidth can be lost by inefficient implementation.

File and Memory Management

Early time-sharing systems had very limited high-speed memories, and much effort was perforce devoted to arriving at a satisfactory paging policy. A particular problem was the avoidance of thrashing, a situation in which one process would load pages only to have them overwritten by another process before it could make any effective use of them. The working-set model developed by Denning proved fruitful in understanding this phenomenon and in guiding the development of satisfactory paging algorithms. As high-speed memories got larger, paging problems became less acute, and there was less need for fine-tuning of paging algorithms. However, since that time, high-speed memories have increased in speed by a very large factor, but disk latency has remained much the same. The result is that the solutions arrived at earlier have failed to scale. I shall return to this subject when I come to discuss current research directions.

An innovation introduced in MULTICS at MIT was the system of attaching files to the virtual memory instead of reading from and writing to them in the conventional manner; such files are said to be mapped onto the virtual memory. This creates a different way of life for the programmer and its merit has never been clearly established.

It is sometimes claimed that attachment of files reduces copying overheads, but it is hard to see that there is much to choose between the two systems in this respect. It is true that the contents of an attached file can be modified in place, without it being necessary to copy the whole file. However, if there is a requirement for the original form of the file to be preserved—for example, for restarting purposes—then a copy of it must be made before it is attached.

The problem is not removed by implementing a system—for example, copy-on-write—in which changes to a file are accumulated in temporary storage and not written back into the file until a late stage, since the changes do eventually come to be written back, and a programmer who wishes to preserve the original contents of a file is still under the necessity of making an advance copy.

A similar problem occurs in database systems in which fixed-length records are updated in place. Here the problem is usually met by making the committing of changes an operation that is explicitly called for by the user of the database. My impression is that there is now little interest in providing file attachment as a feature for users of time-sharing systems. It is, in any case, not appropriate when a file server is being used.

Operating systems brought with them the need for memory protection to prevent user programs from interfering with the system and with each other. In response to this need, hardware designers provided two modes of operation, namely, user mode and privileged mode. It was widely felt that something more was needed and the MULTICS system pioneered rings or levels of protection. As a process moved through the rings in an inward direction it acquired access to more segments of memory. This lead was followed by various vendors who provided rings of protection as a feature of their hardware.

However, it eventually became clear that the hierarchical protection that rings provided did not closely match the requirements of the system programmer and gave little or no improvement on the simple system of having two modes only. Rings of protection lent themselves to efficient implementation in hardware, but there was little else to be said for them.

The attractiveness of fine-grained protection remained, even after it was seen that rings of protection did not provide the answer, and led to much work being done on capability systems in which the capabilities were bit patterns recognized by the hardware. Capabilities may be regarded as *tickets* the possession of which gives the right to access a particular resource, in this case a segment of memory. This again proved a blind alley and all modern processors use the simple system of two modes, user mode and privileged mode.

Hardware support for capabilities was essential if the resulting system was to run fast enough to have any chance of being acceptable in practice. I could not, therefore, see any point in work which was done on capability systems implemented entirely in software. I am not here referring to systems in which capabilities in the form of sparse bit patterns are passed from one computer to another across a network.

UNIX and Its History

UNIX has had a complex and strange history. Originating as a system for a PDP-7 with a small address space and used in a research organization, it was developed to run on large minicomputers in a networked environment. It finally emerged as a full-scale competitor to the major proprietary systems, with the advantage—unique among major systems—of being machine-independent. UNIX appealed mostly to users in science and engineering and had, by the mid 1980s, attained a significant presence in that sector. The early personal workstations were designed by minicomputer engineers who were familiar with UNIX. It was natural, therefore, that when they required an operating system, they should look favorably on UNIX. Indeed, they had little option, since there was no other machine-independent operating system obviously available. The availability of UNIX, as an operating system independent of the processor instruction set, was a major factor in enabling workstations with RISC instruction sets to be accepted by the market. UNIX has stood up well to the challenge, and at the present time it is in universal use for personal workstations.

Unfortunately, there were two competing brands of UNIX and not all personal workstations had the same brand. This situation has become worse, not better, as time has gone on. This is because some users were not happy with either of the brands originally available, and some companies did not find it easy to live with the proprietary problems that they both entailed. In consequence, a number of attempts were made to produce a version of UNIX that would be free of proprietary constraints and would achieve dominance, either because it was manifestly superior to any existing variant or because it had overwhelmingly strong industrial backing. None of these attempts has proved successful. All the systems that have resulted have their adherents, with the result that we now have more brands than ever before. If it turns out, in the next few years, that UNIX has run its course, it will be largely because it has been smothered by its variants.

Microsoft have recently introduced a new operating system known as NT, which is obviously targeted at the UNIX market. Like UNIX it is a general-purpose time-sharing system that can be run on a workstation, but it would also be entirely at home in the role of providing a departmental time-sharing system on a large VAX or other minicomputer. It implements threads and in one version—Windows NT—it provides a modern interface to the user. Windows NT pays special attention to user authentication and security, initially to the level of Class C2. The user who creates an object generally becomes its owner and can specify by means of an access-control list how much use other users may make of it. There is a comprehensive system of resource accounting which enables each user to be assigned quotas for memory usage, number of active objects, and processor time. These are all features appropriate to a time-sharing system serving a large and diverse population of users. It is obviously the belief of the designers of NT that such systems will continue to play a major role in the computing world. As a competitor to UNIX a strong appeal of NT will be that it is a new system entirely free from variants, and that moreover it has every prospect of remaining so.

Operating Systems for Personal Workstations

It appears from what I have just said that present thinking—and practice—is that the appropriate operating system for a high-end personal workstation differs in no respect from the traditional operating system developed in the very different environment of large computers and time-sharing. I can see arguments for believing that this is a natural and proper state of affairs. A single-user workstation needs multitasking both so that the user may run background tasks and so that the system may accept information coming in through a network. It can be argued that virtually all of the process-handling facilities, provided in a general-purpose time-sharing system, are needed for these purposes and that virtually nothing could be saved by taking account of the fact that there is a single user only. Similarly, some protection for files must be provided in order to protect the user against himself or against accident and it can be argued, though here I think less convincingly, that a fully certified security system provides what is needed without either getting in the user's way or adding to the overhead of the system. I shall return to this subject later.

A Range of Operating Systems

The powerful personal workstations that I have been considering constitute only a small part of the total range of desktop computers. There are also PCs, laptops, and even smaller computers; these exist in much larger numbers than do large workstations. Most of the low-end computers run MS-DOS or MS-DOS and Windows, while the high-end computers run UNIX. Since from the hardware point of view the computers form a continuous range, this makes an awkward division.

Historically this division is due to the fact that workstations were developed by minicomputer engineers who, as I have explained, turned naturally to UNIX as a system known to them. In any case they could hardly have adopted MS-DOS from the PC world, since it would have lacked features essential to the high-end user—for example file protection and multi-threading—and these users would have been infuriated by the restriction to eight-letter filenames. On the other hand, it was this very simplicity and lack of frills that constituted the real strength of MS-DOS in its own proper sphere.

In a column I wrote for the *Communications of the ACM* in November 1992 I remarked that it would be too much to expect that a single operating system could be found that would be suitable both for powerful workstations and also for laptops, and even smaller computers. I did suggest, however, that as a long-term aim we might hope for a range of operating systems that were, in some sense, compatible or at least friendly to one another. The family relationship between the various operating systems would be close enough to permit the migration up and down the range of files and programs.

There does not appear to be any insuperable difficulty in providing for the migration of files. The full specification of a filing system might include file protection and the retention of a full updating history. In a lower-level system these features might not be provided, but that would not prevent the files themselves from being copied; it would simply mean that some attributes would be lost. Similarly, when a file was being copied in an upward direction, default values for some attributes might have to be supplied. Easy movement of programs in the downward direction would make life easier for application programmers. They would be able to develop applications on a workstation equipped with a full operating system and then package them to run on smaller computers.

In this connection, I might remark that system programmers need more and more to visualize the requirements of application programmers. The idea, originating at Xerox PARC, that they would do good work provided that they were themselves users of the programming environments they created was a fruitful one in its day, but something more is now required.

File Servers and Other Servers

Along with workstations and ethernets came the requirement for servers of various kinds—file servers, print servers, network interface servers, and perhaps compute servers. An easy way to make a server is to take a workstation running UNIX and equip it with the necessary software. However, a full operating system is unnecessary. This along with the need to make servers highly secure and to maximize throughput—or rather to secure a good compromise between throughput and response time—has led to the design of servers becoming a specialized subject. This is particularly noticeable in the case of file servers; here effective and reliable error recovery is of the highest importance and so is file security. Performance is optimized by making use of sophisticated software caching systems.

Research Directions

Structure of an Operating System

In earlier times designers were often attracted by a layered model, often associating the layers of the model with varying degrees of memory protection. Such models if rigidly adhered to tended to lead to systems that ran very slowly. I remember one operating system constructed in this way that was so slow that an extra year of development time was needed to make it acceptably fast.

A widely expressed ideal is that an operating system should consist of a small kernel surrounded by routines implementing the various services that the operating system provides. The intention is that the kernel should contain all the code that needs to be certified as safe to run in privileged mode and that the peripheral routines should run in user mode. When such a system is implemented, it is found that frequent passage in and out of the kernel is necessary and that the overheads involved in doing this make the system run slowly. There is thus an irresistible pressure to put more and more in the kernel. I am driven reluctantly to the conclusion that the small kernel approach to the structuring of an operating system is misguided. I would like to be proved wrong on this.

Recent developments in programming languages have led to modular or object-oriented models. These free programming languages from the limitations of hierarchical scope rules, and as such I regard them as representing a major advance. It has long been recognized that an operating system is not a monolithic program, but is made up of routines for scheduling, handling interrupts, paging, etc. It would lend itself well to modular or object-oriented design and I am aware that such designs are being worked on. I would like to see public identification of the modules and accepted definitions of the interfaces between them.

A modular or object-oriented operating system would be capable of having plugged into it modules implementing a variety of different policies. It would form a valuable tool for the type of experimental research that I shall mention in the section on software performance.

Paging

I remarked above that high-speed memories have increased in speed by a very large factor, but that disk latency has remained much the same. We can no longer rely on disk transfers being overlapped with useful computation. The result is that users of top-end workstations are now demanding enough high-speed memory to hold their long-term working set, so that disk transfers will be reduced in number. This may be a workable solution at the top end, but will hardly solve the problem for users of more modest equipment. We need to look again at policies other than demand paging, even perhaps roll-in/roll-out policies that take advantage of the high serial transfer rates that can be sustained when blocks of contiguous words are transferred.

The problem is to be seen against the background of probable future developments in memory systems. Up until now, memories have been growing larger but not faster. We may expect to see some emphasis put on the development of faster memory systems for use in top-end workstations. Available approaches are via (1) chips optimized for speed rather than capacity, (2) chips designed for streaming, and (3) the exploitation, for caching purposes, of the internal line registers to be found in memory chips. The last two approaches involve software as well as hardware.

Focus on Software Performance

In the parallel field of processor design, recent years have seen a great emphasis placed on the quantitative evaluation of processor performance. This has been done by running benchmarks on processors or on simulated versions of them. Simulation has been important because it has enabled comparative trials to be made of competing architectures—and of rival features in the same architecture—without its being necessary to implement the processors in silicon. The result has been to develop architectures of very great efficiency and to eliminate features which were ineffective, or which overlapped other features without providing any significant advantage.

There has been no move to subject operating systems to a similar penetrating analysis. To do so is the greatest challenge facing operating systems specialists at the present time. It is not an easy challenge; software differs from hardware in very great degree, and it does not follow that, because quantitative methods have been successful in processor design, they will be equally successful in operating system design.

If they do nothing else, measurements make people stop and think. For example, last May a former colleague who now works for a company that is engaged in doing database type work in C++, told me of an experiment in compiling the common libraries and client side of their system on a SPARCstation 10, and also on a 66-MHz 486 running Windows 3.1. In the result the SPARCstation took a little less than 10 minutes and the 486 took 6 minutes. The cost ratio of the two systems was ten to one.

I found this an arresting result. Obviously one should not draw far-reaching conclusions from a single test of this kind. However, following up such a result, and performing further experiments under carefully controlled conditions, cannot fail to lead to a better understanding of what is going on. There is, I know, work being done on the quantitative evaluation of system performance. I hope that more and more research workers will turn to this subject, and I hope that some of them will take the RISC movement in processor architecture as a model.

Single-user Operating Systems

In spite of what I said above, I am far from happy with the assertion that the ideal operating system for a personal workstation differs in no way from an operating system designed to provide a time-sharing service on a minicomputer. I feel that the use of a full-scale multiuser time-sharing system for a personal workstation must be a case of overkill.

One can approach the problem by asking what are the minimum facilities needed to make the user of a personal workstation happy. The philosophy behind this approach is that, if you carry around facilities and features that you do not really need, you incur an unnecessary cost.

In a research environment users are likely to place great stress on the quality of the interactive service they receive; at the same time, they will want to be able to run one or more background tasks. They will also need network facilities for mail and file transfers. In research laboratories, many users like to be able to use other people's workstations at night or when their owners are away, and thus secure extra computing power. In some environments this is undoubtedly an important requirement. The question is whether it could be provided more simply than by running a multiuser time-sharing system, such as UNIX, on all workstations.

Personal users are likely to be very interested in that form of security better called protection or integrity. This will enable them to protect their files and running programs from accidental damage, whether it arises from their own actions or from those of other users. They are less likely to be interested in secrecy. In fact, many scientific users, especially in universities, see no need for secrecy and would be apprehensive that a system which emphasized it would prevent them from doing many things that they want to do.

The Oberon system, distributed by Niklaus Wirth from ETH Zurich, comprises a language and an operating system, both designed on the lean principles for which Wirth is well known. Those who feel that there may be a future for lean operating systems would do well to examine Oberon.

Program Optimization by an Operating System

There are various simple ways by which an operating system, or rather an operating system and a compiler working together, could use information from earlier runs to optimize a program automatically. For example, it might cause a record to be kept of the number of times the various branches in the program were taken, and then modify the source code so as to minimize this number. This could be regarded as a form of branch prediction based on experience with that particular program, rather than on general program statistics. Similarly, an operating system might keep track of the way that paging occurred and modify the code so that appropriate prefetching took place and so that frequently activated code was retained in memory. Clearly there are issues here affecting the language designer, the operating system designer, and perhaps the hardware designer also.

I pointed out in Essay 8 that, in optimizing a program to run on parallel hardware, the programmer must rely heavily on experience accumulated during earlier runs. I would like to feel that there is a role for the operating system to play in this process.

References

Hopper, A. and R.M. Needham. "The Cambridge Fast Ring Networking System." *IEEE Trans. on Comp.*, vol. 37, no. 10 (1988), p. 1214.

Organick, Elliott Irving. "Multics System: An Examination of Its Structure." Cambridge: MIT Press, 1972.

Ritchie, Dennis. "The Evolution of the UNIX Time-Sharing System." *Bell Lab. Tech. Jour.*, vol. 63, no. 8 (Oct. 1984), pp. 1577–93.

Wilkes, M.V. and R.M. Needham. "*The Cambridge CAP Computer and Its Operating System.*" New York: Elsevier–North Holland, 1979.

ESSAY TWELVE

Artificial Intelligence as the Year 2000 Approaches

I am aware that I have acquired a reputation for being critical of the claims made for artificial intelligence. It is true that I am repelled by some of the hype that I hear and by the lack of self-criticism that it implies. However, the underlying philosophical questions have long been of deep interest to me. I can even claim to be the first AI professional, my definition of a professional being someone who performs a service and accepts a fee in return. I had read Alan Turing's paper "Computing Machinery and Intelligence" which appeared in *Mind* in 1950. I was deeply impressed. Without attempting to emulate Turing's erudition—or the wit in which he clothed it—I wrote a short article on the same subject and offered it to the editor of *The Spectator*, a British journal devoted to contemporary affairs. The editor accepted it and I duly received a fee.

I still consider that, apart from his mathematical papers, the paper in *Mind* is the best thing that Turing ever wrote. He began with the question "Can machines think?" In that form, he found the question to be unsatisfactorily formulated. An attempt to extract the essential underlying point of interest led him to propose the famous Turing test. Instead of asking whether a particular machine could think, he suggested that one should ask instead whether it could pass this test. The test involved the machine posing as a human being and defying an interrogator to detect the imposture.

Turing admitted that he had no strong arguments to put forward in favor of the view that a digital computer would one day be able to pass his test, although he inclined to the view that it would. He made the interesting suggestion that the machine might be equipped with a learning program and taught like a child. The way he put it was that the machine might be programmed to simulate a child's brain rather than an adult's brain. This brings out the point that thinking is intimately connected with learning. Turing was quite aware that the education of a machine would, like that of a child, be a long-drawn-out process. He also saw practical difficulties. The computer would not have legs and could not be sent to school like a normal child. Even if this deficiency could be got over by "clever engineering" he was afraid that the other children might make excessive fun of it!

There is no difficulty in writing a program that will exhibit a simple form of learning, for example, learning to recognize abbreviations for people's names. The program would contain a list of the abbreviations it already understood. Given an unfamiliar abbreviation it would make a guess. It would be told whether it was right or wrong, and would update its list accordingly. This can fairly be called learning, although there is nothing deep about it.

Stimulated by Turing's paper, my colleagues and I tried our hands at writing various learning programs of the kind I have just described. Their limitations soon became obvious. They did what they had been written to do, but no more. For that reason, they were uninteresting as soon as they had been run for the first time. I soon appreciated that a breakthrough was required in the direction of what I called *generalized learning programs* which would go on learning new things.

If computers had existed in the late seventeenth century and people had known how to write generalized learning programs, then a machine equipped with such a program would have been ready to absorb the work of Newton when it was published, and in due

Turing's Dream

Interrogator:	In the first line of your sonnet which reads "Shall I compare thee to a summer's day" would not "a spring day" do as well or better?
Witness:	It wouldn't scan.
Interrogator:	How about "a winter's day?" That would scan all right.
Witness:	Yes, but nobody wants to be compared to a winter's day.
Interrogator:	Would you say Mr. Pickwick reminded you of Christmas?
Witness:	In a way.
Interrogator:	Yet Christmas is a winter's day, and I do not think Mr. Pickwick would mind the comparison.
Witness:	I don't think you're serious. By a winter's day one means a typical winter's day, rather than a special one like Christmas.

Turing's Dream—a dialogue with a computer.
The Interrogator is a human being and the Witness is a computer.

course that of Faraday and Einstein; it would now be doing its best with black holes! It would have read the novels of Dickens, and would be able to engage in the sort of half-teasing dialogue that Turing's fertile mind delighted in inventing—for example, about Mr. Pickwick's reminding it of Christmas and whether Christmas Day is a typical winter's day or not (see "Turing's Dream").

At first, I had hoped that, when a sufficient number of simple learning programs had been written, it might be possible to discern what they had in common and, armed with this insight, to write an unrestricted learning program. This did not happen and it soon became clear to me that it would not happen unless a genius were to arise who could turn the whole subject inside

19 *A. L. Samuel's pioneering work on the game of checkers was followed by similar work on chess. Interest in chess-playing programs for their own sake soon began to develop. From 1970 onwards, there have been regular chess tournaments in which the contestants are computer programs instead of humans. The photograph shows Gary Kasparov, the reigning world chess champion, playing Deep Thought, the world champion chess program. This historic encounter, the first of its kind, took place in New York in 1989. The victor was Kasparov.*

(Courtesy of Marilynn K. Yee/NYT Pictures.)

out. To my surprise, others did not immediately take the point. The programs we wrote were the work of two weeks; others went on to write programs taking two years or longer, but with the same result as far as I could see.

The problem is illustrated well by Arthur Samuel's pioneering work on programs for playing checkers. His main interest was in exploring the method of recursive board search later taken up with such success by writers of chess programs, but he was also interested in seeing whether he could make his program learn from its experience and play a better game in the future.

An essential and frequently repeated step in Samuel's program was to ascribe a measure of goodness to a board position. He devised a number of different ways of computing such a measure. Instead of settling for one of these, he used instead a linear combination, with a weight assigned to each measure. He found that he could devise ways in which the weights could be automatically adjusted to optimize performance, but no way in which the program could invent an entirely new measure and add it to the set it already possessed. In other words, he could write a program to deal with mathematical forms, but not with intellectual concepts.

Some very complex learning programs have been written and have been highly impressive when demonstrated to a non-technical audience. They have, however, always turned out to be programs that optimize their performance by modifying their internal state, either by adjusting parameters or by updating data structures.

A high-water mark of interest in spectacular AI programs was reached in 1971 with a program written by Terry Winograd, whose purpose was to control a robot capable of stacking blocks. The robot was simplified down to the bare essentials and was simulated by computer graphics. This was a striking feature at the time, since the use of computer graphics was then rather uncommon. Commands were given to the robot in English and the serious purpose of the program was to try out a novel method of extracting information from English sentences. However, the combined appeal of the graphics and the natural language interface caused the work to be widely acclaimed as a demonstration of machine intelligence.

The problem of generality in AI was discussed from a modern point of view in an interesting paper by John McCarthy entitled "Generality in Artificial Intelligence" and published in the *Communications of the ACM* in 1987. McCarthy was one of the founders of the artificial intelligence field and it was he who coined the name in 1956.

McCarthy identifies two symptoms of lack of generality in AI. One is that a small addition to the idea of a program often involves a complete rewrite, beginning with the data structures. Another is that no one knows how to make a general database of commonsense knowledge that could be used by any program that needed such knowledge. Getting a language for expressing commonsense knowledge, for inclusion in a general database, he regards as the key problem of generality in AI.

Expert Systems and Turing's Dream

Originally the term "artificial intelligence" was used exclusively in the sense of Turing's dream that a computer might be programmed to behave like an intelligent human being. Of recent years, however, AI has come more and more to be used as a label for programs which, if they had not emerged from the AI community, might have been seen as a natural fruit of work with string-processing languages such as COMIT and SNOBOL, and of the work of E. T. Irons on a pioneering syntax-directed compiler. I refer to expert systems.

In simple expert systems, all the knowledge is incorporated by the programmer in the program, as indeed the alternative name *knowledge-based systems* clearly brings out. It is as though a child were taught the multiplication table by having a surgical operation performed on its brain. In more elaborate expert systems, some updating of an internal database takes place during the lifetime of the system. These systems exhibit the same form of learning as the programs discussed earlier, and have the same limitations. Expert systems are indeed a valuable gift that the AI community has made to the world at large, but they have nothing to do with Turing's dream.

Turing predicted that his dream would be realized within fifty years and moreover that it would be realized on a computer with 128 Mbytes of memory altogether. Fifty years from 1950 brings us to the year 2000 and it is clear that Turing's prediction will not be realized. Indeed, it is difficult to escape the conclusion that, in the forty-odd years that have elapsed since 1950, no tangible progress has been made towards realizing machine intelligence in the sense that Turing envisaged it. The time has perhaps come to face the possibility that it never will be realized with a digital computer.

We use the term "digital computer" to describe the computers we build, although in fact a true digital computer is an abstraction. Any real digital computer must be composed of analog circuits. Turing realized this and indeed it was very apparent to anyone of his period who witnessed the struggles of engineers who were trying to make vacuum-tube circuits behave in a digital manner. The results were only just good enough, as was shown by the tendency of the very early digital computers to make occasional mistakes. At the basic circuit level, engineers still need to recognize that what they design are fundamentally analog devices, and they make routine use of analog simulators and other analog design tools.

A digital computer perforce works within a logical system, and it is known that within such a system there are things that cannot be done. We do not need to evoke Goedel's theorem to prove this; Desargues' theorem about triangles in perspective will do. However, I am not sure of the relevance of arguments at these levels.

On a practical level, the fact that there are limitations to what digital computers can do is illustrated by their inability to solve differential equations directly. The usual way round this difficulty is to replace the differential equation by a difference equation. Unfortunately, difference equations and differential equations are creatures of quite distinct species, and have different properties. For example, a second-order linear differential equation with two-point boundary conditions has an infinite number of independent solutions, whereas the corresponding difference equation has a finite number. This is a difference of kind which cannot be removed by going to a smaller interval in the argument.[9] One of its practical consequences is that parasitic solutions intrude themselves and plague the life of the numerical analyst. Parasitic solutions are artifacts that arise purely and simply from the replacement of the differential equation by a difference equation. The mathematician can make the difference equation and the differential equation come together by proceeding to a limit, but this does not help the worker in the numerical domain for whom limits are not accessible.

The Brain: Digital or Analog?

If we are prepared to regard the human brain as a machine, then we have an existence proof that machines can exhibit intelligence. However, this will not help with the problem of whether digital computers can exhibit intelligence unless we are prepared to assert that the human brain is digital in action. If we do this, we are faced by a purely practical consideration. The human neuron is about 5 orders of magnitude slower than the gates in a modern digital computer; how would it be possible for the brain, if it were digitally organized, to be sufficiently fast? Those who think of the brain as digital will usually say that it must make up for what it lacks in speed by possessing a high degree of parallelism. However, massively parallel computers find it hard to gain a factor of 100 or even 10 in speed by being parallel. Even the most determined enthusiast for parallel computation may balk at a factor of 100,000.

The above argument is, however, academic since there is no reason whatever why we should regard the human brain as a digital device. Indeed, the digital versus analog dichotomy is wholly inappropriate as an approach to the functioning of the human brain. The digital computer is, as I have pointed out, an abstraction—one which a human designer finds useful as a way of organizing his thoughts. There is no reason why a non-human designer should have gone the same way. On the evolutionary hypothesis, it is even an error to regard the brain as having been designed to meet a stated requirement. "Blind evolution stumbled on . . . . lo! there were men and men could think." Function and structure evolved together.

I would suggest that the section of the AI community which is interested in rivaling the action of the human brain would do well to include some analog element in its machines. I am without great enthusiasm for neural nets, but I nevertheless observe that neural nets can include analog discriminating circuits.

I do not wish to give the impression that I think that one day Turing's dream will come true, but with analog rather than digital machines. I make no such prediction. It may indeed be that the sort of analog machines that we are able to construct are themselves subject to limitations, which may or may not parallel those of digital machines. I do, however, suggest that we should take as a working hypothesis that intelligent behavior in Turing's sense is outside the range of the digital computer.

A negative principle can be of great value in guiding research. If it were not for the First Law of Thermodynamics, all bright students of mechanical engineering would want to work on perpetual motion! A recognition that Turing's dream is not going to be realized with a digital computer would perhaps help students avoid unpromising lines of research.

References

Griswold, R.E. and D.R. Hanson. "String Processing." In *Encyclopedia of Computer Science*, 3rd ed., eds. Anthony Ralston and Edwin D. Reilly. New York: Van Nostrand Reinhold, 1993.

Irons, E.T. "A Syntax Directed Compiler for ALGOL 60." *Comm. ACM*, vol. 4, no. 1 (1961), p. 51.

McCarthy, John. "Generality in Artificial Intelligence." *Comm. ACM*, vol. 30, no. 12 (1987), pp. 1030–5. Reprinted in *ACM Turing Award Lectures: The First Twenty Years*. New York: ACM Press, 1987.

Samuel, Arthur L. "Some Studies in Machine Learning Using the Game of Checkers." *Computers and Thought*, eds. Edward A. Feigenbaum and Julian Feldman. New York: McGraw-Hill, 1963, pp. 71–105.

Turing, Alan M. "Computing Machinery and Intelligence." *Mind*, vol. 59 (1950), pp. 433–60.

Turing, Alan M. "Machine Intelligence." Originally submitted to National Physical Laboratory, 1948. Reprinted in *Machine Intelligence 5*, eds. Bernard Meltzer and Donald Michie. New York: Wiley, 1970, pp. 3–23.

Winograd, T. *Understanding Natural Language*. New York: Academic Press, 1972.

ESSAY THIRTEEN

Software and Industrial Research

Industrial research in the modern sense may be said to have its origins in the great inter-war industrial research laboratories, especially the Bell Telephone Laboratories, then in New York, and the GEC Research Laboratories (now known as the Hirst Research Centre) at Wembley in England. The function of these laboratories was the application of the experimental scientific method to industrial problems. They differed greatly from the inventors' workshops of an earlier generation, particularly in regard to the scientific qualifications of the people they employed. An important outcome of their work was the acquisition of patents which could either be exploited directly or licensed to other companies. Money spent on research was seen as being a profitable investment in the purely financial sense.

My first visit to the GEC Wembley Research Laboratories was in the 1930s when I was still a student. It was at a time when the increase in automobile traffic had led to a need for better road lighting and, in particular, for lighting fittings that would produce a uniform level of illumination on the road. This required improved lens design, and we were shown an experimental setup in which the intensity of the light emitted from a fitting could be measured as a

20 *The Research Laboratories of the General Electric Company, Ltd. (now known as the Hirst Research Centre) at Wembley, near London. The photograph of the exterior was taken soon after the Laboratories were opened in 1923. The interior view is that of a laboratory devoted to electric lamp testing.*

(Courtesy of the General Electric Company, Ltd.)

function of angle. Photocells were then high technology and measurement was regarded as a hallmark of the scientific method.

As the computer industry has become dominated by software, hardware research has receded into the background. In consequence, the model of industrial research just described, while still valid in many industries, must be applied with caution in the computer industry. Software research makes no demands for laboratory facilities of the traditional kind nor for people with qualifications in the experimental sciences. It is necessary to have people with original minds and an interest in industrial innovation, but the skills they need are essentially the same as those needed by software engineers or computer scientists generally.

Apart from computer applications, in which I include circuit simulators and other computer design tools, software research in the computer community centers on the following topics: basic programming methodology; programming languages; display software and software associated with workstations; system software, in particular operating systems and programming environments; and file servers and databases.

The computer industry sees itself as advancing as a whole, with industrial research laboratories and university laboratories both contributing to innovation. There is keen competition between companies to recruit the more creative computer science and engineering graduates and to provide them with an environment in which they can develop their talents for the benefit of the company. They are encouraged to take an interest in long-range topics in cooperation with colleagues in universities and other companies. While most such work has limited relevance to the business of a particular company, it is nevertheless important in providing a vehicle by which the more productive members of the research staff may establish links with their opposite numbers in other companies and in universities. Without such links, a research organization rapidly becomes inward looking and unable to fulfill one of its most important roles, namely that of alerting the company at an early stage to incipient trends and developments that may impact its product strategy.

Product designers charged with the short-term evolution of product lines also establish external links, but these tend to be with a different sector of the computer community. Product designers need to keep themselves fully aware of what is happening in their own particular markets, and be prepared to meet competition as they see it developing. Their view of the industry is very different from the longer term view seen by research engineers, but both are valid and one complements the other.

Transfer of technology from outside a company to within it is an important function of an industrial research organization. Many industrial research projects are aimed specifically at importing and acclimatizing technology developed elsewhere. This function is just as important as that of doing innovative research and is likely to absorb the greater part of the effort of an industrial research organization.

A characteristic of the computer industry is that advances in software that directly affect a user must, if they are to be successful, be adopted by the industry generally. Research is conducted with a degree of openness that it would be surprising to find in other areas. This is possible in part because the transfer of software technology is not easily brought about even to one's friends. They as well as competitors need time and experience to become comfortable with new ideas. The research ultimately benefits the industry as a whole. In the short term, the company that has invested in it, and believes in it, can hope to profit first. If a company attempts to exploit the result of the research in an exclusive manner, by being unwilling to release the relevant software, under license or otherwise, it runs the risk of losing this advantage. Anyone who has observed the computer industry over a period of time will be able to point to examples of this happening.

New ideas in operating systems, programming languages, and software tools undergo a long period of gestation and evolution before they either fall by the wayside or become incorporated into accepted practice. The process proceeds slowly. If one looks back over a period of five years, one is hardly conscious of progress taking place at all. One has to look back over a much longer period in order to appreciate fully the radical innovation and change that has in fact occurred.

A Switch to Software Research

In computer hardware, we have now reached the point at which basic research is becoming a specialized art and needs substantial resources. Increasingly, vice-presidents of corporate research in many companies are questioning whether it is any longer appropriate for their particular companies to engage in such research. Some have decided, as a matter of strategic policy, to switch resources to basic research in software. In doing this, they are motivated in part by the concern they feel for the difficulties faced in software production and by the clear need to make it more rapid, more sure, and more predictable. They feel that research on software tools may lead to a solution of these problems. The result is that clean rooms and other experimental facilities are torn out and replaced by cubicles for workstations.

This maneuver is sound if viewed as a contribution to an industry-wide endeavor. It is sound also if the aim is the comparatively modest one of creating a strong support group that will help software developers acquire the software tools that they need—tools that are as advanced as the state of the art permits, or hopefully a little beyond. The policy is dangerous, however, if the problem of developing software tools is approached in idyllic ignorance of the long history of struggles to achieve significant advances in this area, and if a major breakthrough is expected on a time scale of five years or less. The situation also has its dangers for the software engineers engaged in such research. They may well find themselves caught in a career trap created by the wide mismatch between what is expected by their management and what they can possibly deliver.

Collaboration in Research

Much emphasis is now being placed on research conducted in collaboration by groups owing allegiance to otherwise independent organizations.

In the U.S., companies were, until recently, inhibited from entering into collaborative research agreements by fear of antitrust proceedings. The situation was materially changed by the passage of two acts of Congress, namely, the National Cooperative Research Act of 1984 and the Technology Transfer Act of 1986. As a result, cooperative research organizations are now to be found within the computer industry. These organizations have been created by the participating companies themselves, the role of the government having been confined to the passage of enabling legislation. One of the first cooperative organizations to be set up was the Open Software Foundation, through which the cooperating companies hoped to create what would become a common software basis for future products in the industry as a whole. This is a recognition of the fact, noted in the preceding section, that software advances must be adopted generally if they are to achieve their full impact.

Collaboration in research is useful when, as in the above cases, it enables resources to be pooled; in some sciences, such as the earth sciences, international collaboration is essential if certain kinds of research are to be undertaken at all.

Aside from the expectation of reaping the fruits of the research itself, there are various reasons why a company should choose to engage in collaborative research; for example, it may desire to encourage technology transfer or to promote good relations with other governmental or non-governmental organizations.

Within the European Economic Community, research sponsorship has been used as a means of bringing together the separate European countries, and attempting to rectify what was rightly perceived to be an uneven distribution of technological expertise. For example, under the ESPRIT program, which is the principal program under which the European Commission supports research in the computer industry, grants are made, not to individual institutions, but to *ad hoc* consortiums of companies and universities drawn from different European countries. Typically, there are four or five participants, of which one or two may be universities. Universities are funded to the extent of 100% and companies to the extent of 50%.

However, if objectives that are not research objectives are allowed to influence genuine research projects, the quality of the research is likely to suffer. My observations lead me to conclude that in the software area it is especially difficult to combine the achieving of a high standard of research with the attainment of these objectives. While the ESPRIT initiative has been very successful in bringing the European nations closer together and in spreading technological expertise, it has, in my judgement, been less successful in promoting research of high quality.

At the highest level, the ultimate aim of research is to change people's mindsets. This is not assisted by formal collaboration on equal terms with other researchers, however worthy, who do not share the same vision. There is a very grave danger that forcing collaboration in order to achieve some objective unconnected with the research itself will have the effect of blunting the sharp edge of innovation.

Much remains to be learned about the proper management of collaborative research undertakings. The central problem is that of ensuring that the work being done remains relevant as the future unfolds. This is especially the case with innovative research. Flexibility is of the essence in research, and much money can be wasted if a research program is set in contractual concrete at the beginning and pursued unchanged through thick and thin. Unfortunately, when major changes to a project become necessary, it may be difficult for the parties to agree on what they should be, and in the extreme case, even more difficult for them to agree on cancellation.

PART FOUR

Communications

ESSAY FOURTEEN

Computer Networks and the Bandwidth Famine

Data transmission first began to be a subject of general discussion in the computer field in 1960. Earlier, there had been military interest centered on the SAGE project for air defense, but this project had been kept strictly under wraps and few people knew about it. My own interest in data transmission began when I attended a conference in Delft in the Netherlands in September 1960. This was organized by the Institute of Radio Engineers, which was then the leading institute concerned with computer hardware; a few years later it was to join forces with the American Institute of Electrical Engineers to form the present IEEE. Interest in data transmission grew rapidly and received a stimulus from the development of time-sharing in 1963. Since then there has been steady progress towards better reliability and wider bandwidths.

At first doubts were felt about the adequacy for data transmission of contemporary telephone lines. It was feared that they would turn out to be too noisy and too liable to interruption. At Delft, statistics were quoted for noise on telephone lines and there was much speculation about its various causes. It was clear that a good deal of the noise was caused by maintenance work being done in cable ducts and elsewhere. It was noted that the Hawaii cable, which lay undisturbed at the bottom of the ocean, was relatively noise-free. One speaker remarked that, if only the maintenance men would keep out of the way, the situation would be improved!

However, it soon appeared that early fears about the inadequacy of telephone lines were exaggerated and that, by the use of error-control techniques based on redundancy, even noisy lines were perfectly usable, and could in fact be made to yield as low an error rate as was necessary. The effect of noise was to reduce the rate of transmission, not to make the circuit unusable.

Telephone lines have improved over the years, and mechanical switching has given way to electronic switching. A modern adaptive modem can squeeze a great deal of bandwidth out of a voice-grade line. Further improvements in the quality of telephone lines may be expected. These will be welcome for data, but will probably not be noticed by the ordinary telephone user.

Wide Area Networks

General-purpose computer networks go back to the ARPANET, the building of which was begun in 1969. The ARPANET was first described at a major conference in 1970, when L. G. Roberts and B. D. Wesler presented a paper entitled "Resource Sharing Computer Networks" to the Spring Joint Computer Conference. At that time, software systems were not nearly as portable as they have since become, and there were major difficulties in transferring a system from one computer to another. The solution proposed was to leave the system where it was and to make it possible to use it remotely from other sites. This was one of the main motivations for establishing the ARPANET. In consequence, the ARPANET emphasized remote login facilities, together with facilities for transferring files from one computer to another. At the time of the conference in 1970 the ARPANET had twenty stations on it.

The ARPANET was a resource-sharing computer network. Another network, established at about the same time, but initially for the more limited role of providing access to a proprietary time-sharing service, was the Tymnet. This was described at the Spring Joint Computer Conference in 1971. It had many innovative features and has not received the recognition it deserves.

When first proposed the ARPANET was staggering in its boldness. For example, it made use of leased lines of 56 kilobits/sec bandwidth. Using such a bandwidth was then unheard of. It was reported that the telephone company at first said that they had no tariff for such a thing and that ARPA found it necessary to apply the superior persuasive powers of the U.S. government. No doubt, in the fullness of time, large-scale resource-sharing networks were bound to come. What Roberts and his associates did was to telescope the time interval—they made the clock go round faster.

The ARPANET consisted of a network of computers known as IMPs (interface message processors) used solely for switching. They were under central control, and their programs were loaded using the network itself. The working computers, known as hosts, were connected to the IMPs. There was thus an independent communication network with hosts attached to it. The bandwidths of the leased lines and the switching capacity of the IMPs were together fully sufficient to ensure that, under all normal traffic conditions, the transmission time across the network for a 1-Kbyte packet would not exceed 0.5 second, its planned maximum value. Since the communication network was independent of the hosts, there was nothing a local site manager could do to disturb this.

It came to me as a surprise—no doubt I had not sufficiently taken economic considerations into account—to find that the later computer networks that grew up did not follow the same principle. Instead, they were formed by the direct interconnection of the host computers. Message switching became a part-time function of the operating system in each of the hosts; this included the forwarding of messages in transit to other hosts. The efficient working of the network was thus dependent on the state of loading of the hosts and on the good will of the site managers. If a host was taken out of service for local reasons, the network was impaired by the loss of that node, which could well be an important one. It is surprising that these networks worked as well as they did. Their performance improved as host computers became more powerful and more reliable. At the same time, the user community began to attach increased importance to network services, and this change was reflected in a changed attitude on the part of the site managers responsible for the nodal computers.

A typical site is now likely to comprise groups of computers, each group having its own local ethernet. The ethernets are connected by a *router* to the wider network, and this router functions much in the manner of an IMP on the ARPANET. Thus, to some extent, the situation may be said to have righted itself.

By the late 1960s a demand for lines of wider bandwidth began to make itself felt. This demand continued to grow and was more than could be met. The result was a bandwidth famine which has continued, with some recent relaxation, to the present day. It has been a true famine in the sense that it has not been possible to acquire enough bandwidth for all purposes, however much one was prepared to pay.

Local Area Networks

Up to the middle 1970s, the computer community was content to use the telephone company's offerings for local areas as well as for wide areas. Around this time, the ethernet was announced and interest in rings for data communication was revived. From the beginning both approaches emphasized wide bandwidths, which were achieved as a natural consequence of using computer engineering techniques in place of telecommunication techniques.

The ethernet created for itself an ecological niche into which it exactly fitted, its capabilities and its limitations closely matching what the community could use. The contention principle, on which it was based, appealed to people's imagination and the bandwidth was more than adequate for the time. Limitation to a relatively small geographical area was not seriously felt.

The overwhelming attraction of the early ethernets and rings was their simplicity. They were not networks in the true sense although the term local area network was early adopted. They were one-level interconnect systems, with flat addressing and no routing problems. As soon as ethernets (or rings) are interconnected to give a genuine network, simplicity vanishes and all, or nearly all, of the problems associated with wide area networks come rushing in. This is particularly true if the resulting local area network is multiply connected. However, present methods of interconnecting ethernets, while not without their problems, are perfectly adequate for current requirements.

LANs will inevitably move to wider bandwidths, and it is beginning to become clearer how this may happen. Ethernets have already reached their potential. Rings operating in the range 50–100 Mbits/sec have been in use for some time and a standard (FDDI) exists. There are already experimental versions of rings operating in the gigabit/sec range.

The use of fiber-optic cables as the transmission medium enables rings to cover a wide geographical area—well beyond a local area as that term is usually understood. However, large rings are unwieldy and packets take a long time to go round. Rings are perhaps best adapted for use in a backbone interconnect role. A recent development is the growth of interest in LANs based on VLSI crosspoint switches. At one time it had seemed that VLSI was not well adapted to the fabrication of crosspoint switches, because of the large number of pins required. This problem is now in the past and VLSI crosspoint switches are available commercially.

How to interleave long and short messages has long been a central problem in the design of both local and wide area networks. Currently, the favored solution is to divide the messages into fairly short *cells* of fixed size, each containing header bytes, error-control bytes, and data bytes. This is known as asynchronous transfer mode, abbreviated to ATM. A cell containing 53 bytes of which 48 are used for data has been adopted as standard. ATM can be used for both the long- and short-haul sections of a network, and can even extend inside computer equipment.

In the past, engineers from the telecommunications and computing worlds have tended to look at data transmission from very different angles, but they agree on the merits of ATM; in consequence, it is making rapid progress.

The decision as to what should be located centrally, and what should be located in the user's office, depends on the speed of the LAN and on its reliability. On a practical level, there is an obvious advantage in locating, in a central computer room, equipment that is noisy, gives off heat, and requires maintenance. Installing workstations in an office building can lead to expenditure on enhanced air conditioning that exceeds the cost of the workstations themselves. As LANs move to higher speeds, it will become possible, if so desired, to separate the display processing from the display itself. All that the user would then need to have on his desk would be the bare display hardware. On a more technical level, opinion on centralization has swung from side to side as users have weighed the advantages of independence against the value of central services.

Current Developments

Long-distance data transmission is also getting faster. This is largely as a result of the coming into use on a wide scale of fiber-optic cables. The use of pulse-code modulation by telephone companies has made a data rate of 64 Kbits/sec the norm for a voice channel, although at present the ordinary subscriber does not see those bits; what he gets is an analog voice-grade connection. Leased circuits of 1 Mbit/sec are no longer uncommon, and even higher bit rates are coming into use. We may expect dramatic improvement in the availability and cost of wide-bandwidth rented lines as the long-haul data business becomes more competitive. It is not too much to hope that we are moving away from a famine situation towards something approaching a free market situation in which those prepared to pay a reasonable charge will be able to get what they need.

New activities, based on wide-band digital technology, are growing up all the time. Not all of them make demands on telecommunications bandwidth. For example, we are witnessing the birth of a new industry seeking to exploit the enormous storage capacity of CD-ROMs, a data version of the familiar compact discs used for audio recording. It was reported in August 1994 by Dataquest Inc. that nearly 7 million CD-ROM disk drives for PCs were shipped in 1993. They estimated that between two and three times as many would be shipped in 1994. The *Oxford English Dictionary* has been available in CD-ROM form for some time, and it has been

21 *The Oxford English Dictionary is available in two forms, one a set of printed volumes and the other a CD-ROM.*

(Courtesy of Oxford University Press.)

22 *Video on a workstation. Photographs taken in early 1990 of the Pandora project at the Olivetti Research Laboratory in Cambridge, England. (top) An experimental workstation installed in an office. (bottom) A close-up of the screen as seen by the user. This includes several X-windows, one of which contains a digitized video image of a person in another office with whom the user is working. A smaller window contains an image of the user himself and a copy of this image is being transmitted to the remote user. Underlying the two windows is a window containing a computer program written in C. When the Pandora system was designed, it was necessary to have a separate box, external to the workstation, to mix the video images with the normal workstation output. High performance workstations now have sufficient bandwidth to make this unnecessary.*

(Courtesy of Olivetti Research Laboratory.)

possible to exploit its resources in new and imaginative ways. For example, whereas formerly it was only possible to access an entry under its headword, it is now possible to search for keywords within the entries themselves. CD-ROMs can also be used to store digitized video, and before very long it will be possible for the public to buy its television entertainment in that form.

Parallel developments are taking place in computer research laboratories. It is not uncommon to see a television image displayed in a window on a workstation, while other windows display text, graphics, programs, and data in the usual way. At first, the television pictures were in analog form and were incapable of being manipulated by the processor. However, digital representation is now usual and this opens up endless possibilities for the editing and merging of images. Desktop editing of images may become an important computer application in the way that desktop publishing has done. Since the borderline between editing an image for legitimate reasons and editing it for purposes of misrepresentation is not easy to draw, these developments are likely to present lawmakers and judges with some interesting challenges.

Coming into use are databases for personnel records in which biographical summaries along with a digital photograph can be displayed on a computer terminal. Some years ago, one of my colleagues in the Olivetti Research Laboratory in Cambridge, England, showed me such a database with a difference. An entry for one of my old friends was turned up and a picture of him was displayed. I was not particularly impressed, until suddenly the man in the picture began to move. The effect on me was electric! It was no longer just a picture; it was the man himself. Without seeing this demonstration, I would not have believed that motion could add so much value to a photograph.

We may undoubtedly expect to see, alongside computer documents of the kind we know today, a new kind of document in which text, voice, and images will be integrated. Whether the use of such multimedia documents will become widespread, or whether their use will be confined to certain restricted applications is not yet clear.

Advances in telecommunications, the use of optical fibers in particular, will provide plenty of bandwidth for traditional computer networking with its emphasis on resource sharing. The major growth, however, will be in bulk data traffic, arising from the supercomputing world, from NASA, and from similar sources. This will also be reference material and multimedia documents. Much of this latter traffic will be related to information sharing, rather than to computing.

The networks we now have were designed for traditional computer traffic with its emphasis on slick handling of short messages. If bulk data traffic were allowed to flood in, these networks would become unusable for their original purpose. At one time it appeared that the solution would be to build separate networks, specially optimized for bulk data; indeed such networks may well come into existence for handling traffic that is not closely related to computing. However, it now seems likely that the adoption of asynchronous transfer mode as the underlying transport mechanism will enable networks to be designed that can handle both traditional computer traffic and also bulk data traffic. Optical fibers can be relied on to provide the necessary raw bandwidth to support such networks.

References

ARPANET. "THE ARPA Network." (Comprises five papers.) *Proc. AFIPS Spring Joint Computer Conference*, 1972, pp. 243–98.

Hopper, A. and R.M. Needham. "The Cambridge Fast Ring Networking System." *IEEE Trans. on Comp.*, vol. 37, no. 10 (1988), p. 1214.

Lane, J. "ATM Knits Voice, Data on Any Net." *IEEE Spectrum*, vol. 31, no. 2 (1994), pp. 42–5.

Roberts, L.G. and B. D. Wesler. "Computer Network Development to Achieve Resource Sharing." *Proc. AFIPS Spring Joint Computer Conference*, 1970, pp. 543–49.

Wilkes, M.V. "The Impact of Wide Band Local Area Communication Systems on Distributed Computing." *IEEE Computer*, vol. 13, no. 9 (1980), p. 22.

Wilkes, M.V. "Data Transmission and the New Outlook for the Computer Field." *Comp. Jour.*, vol. 4 (1961), pp. 1–9.

ESSAY FIFTEEN

Email and Its Competitors

It often happens that imaginative initiatives, especially when they are on a large scale, have unforeseen outcomes. Indeed, this is one of the main reasons for conducting research in computer systems. The way in which email on the ARPANET was embraced by the user community, and rapidly became of major importance is a case in point.

From the beginning, time-sharing computers had a feature whereby users might send messages to one another, and the designers of the ARPANET must have realized that it would be possible to send messages across the net.[10] However, there is no reference to this possibility in the paper by Roberts and Wesler published in 1970, nor is there any in a subsequent group of papers presented to the Spring Joint Computer Conference two years later in 1972. It may have seemed that the sending of messages would be a misuse of a costly computer network and that even to mention it when making a case for a major financial investment would be counter-productive. Nevertheless, after a very few years, almost everyone connected to the ARPANET made use of the mail facilities and was enthusiastic about them. There were soon many users who rarely used any of the other facilities of the ARPANET. People in the ARPANET community whose work was mainly administrative, and who traveled around the country, found email invaluable in enabling them to keep contact with their own offices and to do their work wherever they happened to be. I heard a lecture to that effect at a conference in Japan in 1975. It was quite obvious that email on the ARPANET had changed the speaker's life. It was then that I began to appreciate that to use the ARPANET for email and nothing else was not an abuse of its facilities, but rather the contrary.

Email on the ARPANET was user-friendly and it remained so for a long time. In the early 1980s, when the ARPANET had been operating for ten years and contained about 100 nodes, I was working at the Digital Equipment Corporation in Maynard, Massachusetts. I was known on the net as wilkes@digital. What could be simpler?

The ARPANET expanded, other networks were formed, and mail gateways were established between them. Email was no longer confined to the small and privileged community of ARPANET users. Inter-networking brought a host of problems. The new networks were formed of computers linked by leased lines and dial-up lines. The computers were not only required to give a service to their local users, but also to act as switching computers for the network. In many cases they lacked the processing power necessary to do both these things efficiently. The leased lines were mostly of voice grade and frequently formed a bottleneck. Inevitably, delays occurred and queues built up, especially at the gateways.

Sometimes messages failed to be delivered for good reasons, perhaps because the recipient was unknown at the destination. Most networks provided for an explanatory message to be sent to the originator in such circumstances. Unfortunately, there were real difficulties in ensuring that those messages were passed correctly across the mail gateways from one network to another. In consequence, messages for another network were launched into the unknown, with a significant chance that nothing more would be heard of them.

As a result of the strenuous efforts of the network community, the problems just mentioned are now largely in the past. Some difficulties remain in the finding of the appropriate node name on which to reach a prospective addressee, but information services available to users and to postmasters are improving. Especially welcome is the move to introduce standardized form for the name by which users are known. The sooner such a standardized form becomes generally adopted to replace or supplement the varied collection of initials, nicknames, etc. by which users are now known, the better it will be for all concerned.

Fax

Fax is based on the telephone system. The steady improvement of that system—internationally it has been a dramatic improvement—has made fax possible. Equally important have been developments in modems. The most advanced are capable of sending at a speed of 9600 baud if the line is good enough and of automatically choosing a lower speed if it is not. For a time, fax was handicapped by a lack of accepted transmission standards, but once this situation was corrected, the way was open for fax to become a powerful competitor for email.

Fax is compatible with normal office routine, and is easily operated by office staff. With email it is first necessary to teach people how to use a computer. A fax message is addressed to the recipient by name and sent to a fax machine at his or her office, where office staff will see that it is delivered. Finding the fax number is just like finding any other telephone number.

If the distant fax machine is busy, there will be some delay in setting up the connection. Once this has been achieved, however, the message goes through in real time and one can be sure that it has arrived. There is no storage in the network, any necessary queueing taking place at the sending office. This does not prevent delay occurring on account of network congestion or limited capacity at the receiving end, but it does mean that the delay is visible at once to the sender, who can consider what alternative courses are open to him. From the business user's point of view, this gives fax a decisive advantage over those computer networks in which messages are accepted at once, but may be subject to variable and unknown delay before they are delivered. If the delay could be limited to, say, an hour, there would perhaps be no problem. Unfortunately, once delays are allowed to occur in a computer network, there is no known effective way of putting an upper limit on their duration.

The telephone network is suited to the transmission of messages because it is universal, it has a well-developed addressing system that works, its bandwidth is adequate, and, from the point of view of the user, messages go directly to their destination. The telephone company has all the headaches associated with routing, redundancy, upgrading of plant, and so on.

Fax depends on the transmission of scanned images and email depends on the transmission of ASCII characters. These appear to be quite distinct techniques. Nevertheless, there are possibilities for some convergence. For example, it is possible to generate from ASCII text within a computer a scanned image suitable for transmission via a modem to a distant fax machine. Cards for this purpose suitable for plugging into a PC are available on the market. A user with a computer so equipped can draft a message in the usual way and then have the option of sending it either by email or by fax. Some fax machines are capable of accepting information in the form of an ASCII string, making the use of the special card unnecessary.

Current fax machines transmit their information via a modem connected to a regular (analog) telephone line. Machines designed for connection to an ISDN 64 kbit/sec circuit are becoming available; these will be capable of improved performance and will enable further possibilities to be exploited.

There is growing interest in voice-mail, and this may be regarded as another competitor for email. In a sense, voice-mail began when people began to connect telephone answering machines to their telephones. At first, these machines were regarded as providing temporary cover when the user of a telephone was away from his home or office. Now there are many telephone lines to which answering machines are permanently connected, and whose sole role is the receipt of voice-mail. In many hotels, voice-mail is a regular part of the message services provided for guests. Some experiments are in progress with video-mail, in which the message consists of a television image as well as speech.

References

ARPANET. "The ARPA Network." (Comprises five papers). *Proc. AFIPS Spring Joint Computer Conference*, 1972, pp. 243–98.

Roberts, L.G. and B.D. Wesler. "Computer Network Developments to Achieve Resource Sharing." *Proc. AFIPS Spring Joint Computer Conference*, 1970, pp. 543–49.

ESSAY SIXTEEN

Light Amplifiers and Solitons

It is always good to look across into your neighbor's backyard and see what is going on. Just now our colleagues in the telecommunications industry have become excited about the possibility of building long-distance submarine cables with amplifiers instead of repeaters.

The light amplifier is one of the most remarkable inventions of recent years. When you know how to make one, and have the right materials available, it is very simple. Lord Rayleigh made a similar remark about a telephone when he was first shown one in 1882 (see "Lord Rayleigh and the Telephone"). In a light amplifier, the amplification depends on *laser* action, the word "laser," it will be recalled, being an acronym for light amplification by stimulated emission of radiation.

Surprisingly, special fiber is not essential. Regular fiber can provide the laser action. All that is necessary is to inject, at a point where the signal is weak, a strong input from a separate, continuously running semiconductor laser. This input is known as the pump. Its effect is to raise some of the atoms of the glass of which the fiber is composed to an excited (metastable) state, known as a Raman state. The wavelength on which the pump operates—slightly different from that of the signal—is chosen to be efficient for this purpose. The atoms would eventually decay spontaneously but, since they are in a metastable state, this would take some time. In practice,

Lord Rayleigh and the Telephone

Yesterday, I had the opportunity of seeing the telephone which everyone has been talking about. The extraordinary part of it is its simplicity. A good workman could make the whole thing in an hour or two. I held a conversation with Mr. Preece from the top to the bottom of the house with it and it certainly is a wonderful instrument, though I suppose not likely to come much into practical use.

From a letter written from Plymouth in the summer of 1882.
(*Life of Lord Rayleigh by His Son*, London 1924)

the great majority of the excited atoms are acted on by the signal and stimulated to decay. In doing so, they emit radiation which is coherent with the signal, and serves to augment it. As the signal and pump progress along the fiber, energy is progressively transferred from the pump to the signal.

Raman amplification needs a powerful pump and it is better to use fiber doped with a minute amount of erbium. A few meters of this cable is sufficient and much less pump power is needed. It is then possible to make a lumped amplifier, consisting of a tiny semiconductor laser and a small coil of fiber. Such an amplifier can be inserted into the cable wherever gain is required.

Light amplifiers may be expected to find wide application. For example, they will greatly facilitate the use of optical fiber for cable television since, given the availability of an amplifier, the amount of energy it is necessary to bleed off for each subscriber, or group of subscribers, is very small.

Submarine Cables

In telecommunications it is now possible to contemplate the design of submarine cables using amplifiers instead of repeaters. The advantages of doing this are threefold: first, amplifiers are much simpler than repeaters. In the latest transatlantic cable to be laid, the repeaters comprise as many as nine custom bipolar ICs, along with associated supervisory circuits of comparable complexity. Secondly, if wavelength multiplexing is used, a separate repeater must be provided for each channel, whereas an amplifier has sufficient bandwidth to cover all the channels. Thirdly, since the design of the amplifiers does not depend on the modulation method used, upgrading the cable to use a more efficient form of modulation can be done by making changes in the terminal equipment only.

Digital repeaters have the advantage that they remove all noise and jitter; the pulses emerging after 6,000 km are as clean as those that went in. Design problems might be encountered if the cable stretched as far as the moon, but for terrestrial distances there are no problems. With amplifiers, on the other hand, noise builds up. This is not a serious problem over distances of 1,000 km or so. Unfortunately, some of the noise is due to spontaneous decay of atoms from a metastable state and affects phase as well as amplitude. This has a serious effect in the case of very long distance cables, such as those necessary to cross the Atlantic and the Pacific.

A less-expected problem is that, over very long distances, nonlinearity in the fiber makes itself felt. It has long been known that pronounced nonlinear effects are observed if fibers are operated at very high power levels and, as we will see later, work is proceeding with a view to turning these effects to practical advantage. The mild nonlinearity observed at low power levels has various effects, one being cross modulation between the Fourier components of the transmitted pulse. It is surprising that nonlinearity should become important with a power input of only about a milliwatt. The source of the nonlinearity is the Kerr effect. This has long been known and exploited, for example, in the Kerr cell used in light switches in television and similar applications.

The combined result of nonlinearity and amplifier noise is that the spectrum of the emerging pulse is much distorted. It appears that, in the case of very long submarine cables, this distortion may be sufficiently severe to render wavelength multiplexing impracticable. Similarly, it rules out signaling methods, such as phase modulation or coherent detection, that assume preservation of phase.

However, in spite of these problems, the use of amplifiers instead of repeaters remains an attractive proposition. At present there are two transatlantic cables that use digital transmission, TAT-8 laid in 1988 and TAT-9 laid in 1992. These both use repeaters. Two more cables using repeaters are planned, after which it is expected that a change to amplifiers will be made. Similar plans exist for cables across the Pacific. A traffic capacity of 2.5 Gbits/sec is confidently expected, with the possibility of a subsequent increase to 5 Gbits/sec brought about by changing the terminal equipment only.

Nonlinearity as an Ally

For the more distant future there is the interesting possibility of being able to treat nonlinearity as an ally rather than as an enemy. If the pulse shape and amplitude are correctly chosen, the effect of nonlinearity can be to cancel that of dispersion. Very high input powers are required—watts, as compared with about a milliwatt as used in conventional cables. Since a monomode fiber is only some four or five wavelengths in diameter, an optical input of few watts can amount to megawatts per square centimeter.

That nonlinearity can cancel dispersion has long been known in the case of waves in a canal containing water. In 1834 Scott Russell was watching a barge being drawn along the Edinburgh-to-Glasgow canal by a pair of horses. Suddenly the barge was stopped. The water was thrown into some agitation. After a short time a solitary wave of simple form emerged and began to move steadily along the canal. Russell described it as a heap of water. He was able to follow it on horseback at a trot (about 8 mph) for one or two miles before he lost it in the windings of the canal.

Russell realized that if an attempt were made to launch a solitary wave of small enough amplitude for the motion to be linear, dispersion would soon cause the wave to lose its form, and that the stability of the wave he had observed depended on nonlinearity. A number of physicists, including Rayleigh, turned their attention to the theory of nonlinear waves and it fell to two Dutch researchers to give a definitive formulation of the equation governing the propagation of such waves in a shallow canal. This equation is known after them as the Kortweg–de Vries or KdV equation. A general solution of this equation could not at that time be hoped for, but a special solution corresponding to a single solitary wave was obtained. No discussion of the stability of this wave was possible.

Solitary waves in a canal can be of any amplitude. The larger the amplitude, the smaller the width of the wave and the higher its speed. Suppose two solitary waves, a large one and a small one, start out so far apart that they are essentially independent of one another. If the large one is behind, it will eventually catch up and collide with the smaller. In Russell's time no one seemed to have asked what would happen in these circumstances. Certainly no experiments were done. It was probably assumed that the two waves would destroy each other.

It was not until 1964 that numerical calculations revealed the astonishing fact that the large solitary wave passes through the small one almost as though no nonlinearity were present. The only difference is that the large wave emerges slightly ahead of where it would be expected to be, and the small wave lags slightly behind. Waves that behave in this way are called solitons. Here was perhaps the first indication that a nonlinear world is not necessarily a completely mad world. Solitons are like the people one meets in mental institutions—peculiar in some ways, but normal a lot of the time.

In 1967 an analytical solution to the nonlinear KdV equation was obtained (See Figure 23 on page 161.). This was a major mathematical breakthrough and had the effect of putting the subject on a firm theoretical basis. It confirmed the results obtained by numerical experiment and opened the way to theoretical discussion of stability.

Solitons in Optical Fibers

Had the method been applicable only to the KdV equation, it would have been greeted as a remarkable mathematical success, but an isolated one. In fact, the method is of more general application, and has made a welcome addition to the mathematical physicist's arsenal of methods for dealing with nonlinear differential equations. In particular, the method may be applied to the more difficult equation governing waves propagated in an optical fiber. These waves are modulated on to an infrared carrier, whereas the waves in the canal are base band. In spite of this difference, very similar phenomena occur. In particular, if the size and shape of the pulse are correctly related and if there is negligible attenuation, the effect of nonlinearity is to cancel that of dispersion and make the propagation of solitons possible. It was ten years before fiber was available with low enough attenuation for this theoretical prediction to be tested experimentally.

In 1980 L.F. Mollenaur, R.H. Stolen, and J.P. Gorden of AT&T Bell Laboratories announced the results of a landmark experiment using a length of fiber sufficiently short for attenuation to be negligible. They were able to generate pulses of the shape required by the theory. They found that a low power-input pulse of this shape gave rise to an output pulse showing dispersive broadening. As the power was increased the broadening became less, and at a critical power the output pulse was of the same shape and size as the input pulse. In other words, the pulse was a soliton. The observed critical power was in good agreement with that predicted by the theory.

The lengths of fiber used in the experiment were short enough for attenuation to be unimportant. To cause a soliton to be propagated without change of form for any useful

time = -0.5
A fast soliton approaching a slow one.

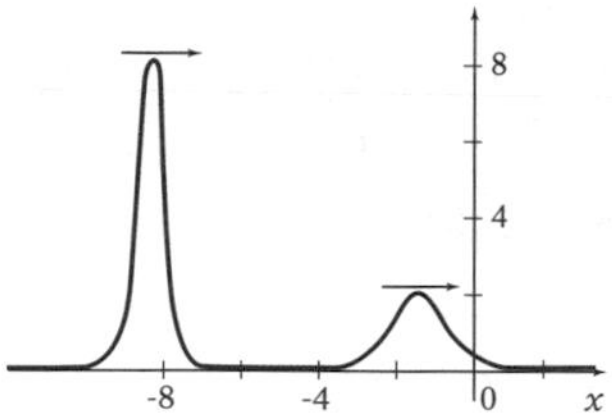

time = -0.1
Beginning of the interaction.

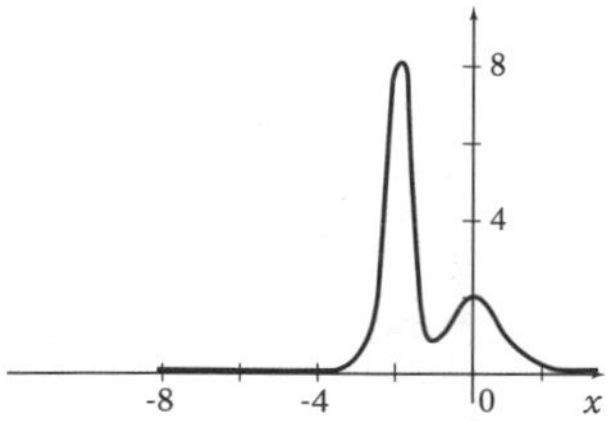

time = 0.0
Solitons merged.

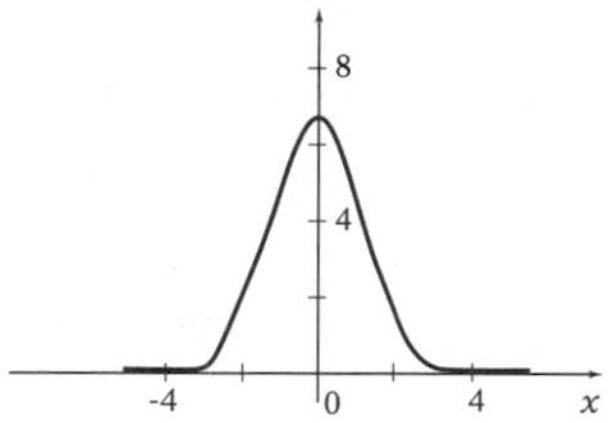

time = 0.1
The fast soliton beginning to emerge.

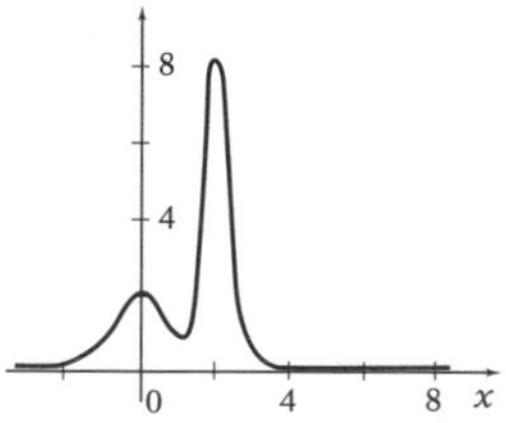

time = 0.5
Leaving the slow one behind.

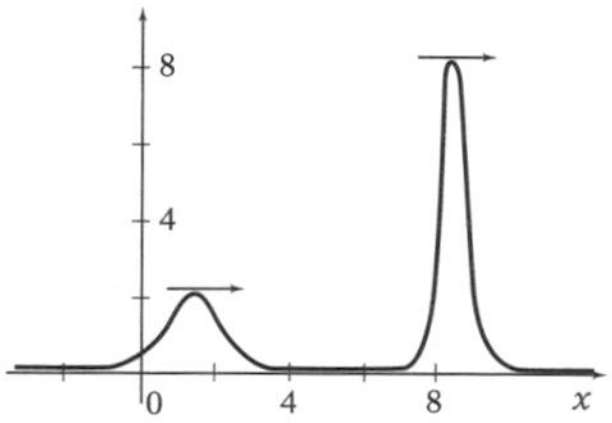

23 *A fast soliton in a canal overtaking a slow one. The curves are computed from an analytical solution of the (non-linear) KdV equation. The fast soliton appears to pass through the slow one just as it would if the equation were linear; however, more detailed plots would show that the fast soliton becomes slightly advanced and the slow one slightly retarded.*

(Redrawn with permission from P. G. Drazin and R. S. Johnson. Solitons: An Introduction. Cambridge: University Press, 1989.)

distance it would be necessary to provide continuous amplification along the length of the fiber, the gain just canceling the loss. This is not practicable, and there is no alternative to the use of lumped amplifiers. Fortunately solitons are remarkably stable and able to stand ill treatment. If the amplifiers are no more than about 30 km apart—corresponding to a 10 db loss—the solitons emerging from each amplifier are restored to their original form. It is necessary that the soliton period, as defined in the next section, should be large compared with the amplifier separation.

Higher Order Solitons

Mollenaur and his colleagues tried increasing the input power above the critical value. They found that the total energy was still concentrated in the same time span, but that most of it was accounted for by a narrow centrally placed peak. Further increases in power resulted in more than one peak developing, the total energy remaining confined as before.

For an input pulse of the critical power, the output is of the same form whatever the length of the fiber, provided it is short enough for attenuation to be negligible. For higher powers, the exact shape and number of peaks depends on the length of the fiber. For input amplitudes that are integral multiples of the critical amplitude, the pulse comes back to its original form after traversing a certain distance along the fiber. It is then referred to as a higher order soliton. These results are in qualitative and quantitative agreement with predictions of the theory.

The distance for the pulse to come back to its original form is known as a soliton period, and is a fundamental distance as far as a particular fiber and a particular soliton width are concerned. The soliton period is proportional to the width of the soliton and inversely proportional to the dispersion coefficient, a property which can be controlled during manufacture of the fiber. By adjusting the dispersion coefficient, the soliton period can be varied from a number of meters to many kilometers.

It is a fortunate fact that optical solitons on the same carrier do not overtake one another in the way that solitons in a canal do. However, if several different wavelengths are used for multiplexing, solitons on different channels will travel at different speeds, since speed depends on carrier wavelength. It is found that they pass each other quite happily without mutual interference provided that they do not overlap when they are launched.

A soliton is sometimes defined as an isolated wave that travels without change of form. However, this is a poor definition since it depends on a property that no real soliton can possess, since significant attenuation must always be present in any real fiber. Moreover, higher order solitons do suffer a change of form although they periodically recover their original form. The important property of solitons is their stability, and the way they can interact with each other without losing their identity. In these respects, solitons behave more like particles than waves.

The Practical Outlook for Solitons

The use of solitons does not overcome the problem of accumulated amplifier noise. Unfortunately, noise due to spontaneous emission can take the form of a small shift in the wavelength of the carrier of a soliton and hence in the speed at which it travels. This causes the soliton to wander in time as it passes through succeeding amplifiers. The resulting jitter—known as Gordon-Haus jitter—builds up in random-walk fashion. It has been found, by numerical solution of the propagation equation, that this wandering of the solitons can be controlled to a useful extent by inserting a bandpass filter after each amplifier. It is one more striking illustration of their particle-like stability that solitons should submit to being disciplined in this way.

A consequence of the jitter is that, over transatlantic distances, a soliton requires a time slot that is up to five times its width. This effectively limits the data rate than can be obtained with solitons to much the same as can be obtained with a conventional system. However, the pulse spectrum of a soliton, as well as its shape, changes little over great distances. Solitons may, therefore, lend themselves better than conventional pulses to wavelength division multiplexing, and this could give them an advantage of as much as a factor of five in data throughput.

It is possible that towards the end of the present decade firm plans will be put in place for laying a cable based on solitons. By then the problems of designing a conventional cable with amplifiers will have become clarified and more will have been learned about solitons and their behavior.

References

Drazin, P.G. and R.S. Johnson. *Solitons: An Introduction*. Cambridge: Cambridge University Press, 1990.

Hasegawa, A. *Optical Solitons in Fibres*. Berlin: Springer-Verlag, 1990.

Haus, H.A. "Molding Light into Solitons." *IEEE Spectrum*, vol. 30, no. 3 (1993), pp. 48–53.

Mollenaur, L.F. "Solitons in Optical Fibres and the Soliton Laser." *Phil. Trans. Roy. Soc. Lond.*, vol. A 315 (1985), p. 437.

Taylor, J.R., ed. *Optical Solitons: Theory and Experiment*. Cambridge: Cambridge University Press, 1992.

PART FIVE

Computer Security

ESSAY SEVENTEEN

Computer Security in the Business World—Time-Sharing Systems

Until recently, most business managers regarded computer security as yet one more charge on their budgets. If pressed they would say that they saw computer penetration as a new way of perpetrating fraud and that pre-existing methods of keeping fraud under control were applicable. The military, on the other hand, have always taken for granted the overriding importance of security. They are particularly concerned to prevent leakage of information, and have tended to see computer security largely in terms of the control of access to classified documents.

A fresh situation was created when networks began to be penetrated by certain mischievous individuals who introduced worms and viruses into them. This led to everyone, both military and civilian, being caught in the grip of a new fear, namely that of data being corrupted and systems disrupted. The attack is no longer carried out by unaided human means. The would-be penetrator writes a program to do his dirty work for him. He must himself identify the weaknesses in the defense, but the program will then probe them remorselessly and at high speed, missing very little.

The simultaneous sharing of computers by many users first brought security problems to the fore. F. Corbató of MIT, and other designers of the early experimental time-sharing systems in universities, recognized the problem and sought to solve it by requiring users to type passwords and by providing codes for file protection. The challenge to break in proved irresistible to the students, and it soon became apparent that improvements were needed both in the design of systems and in their implementation. Roger Needham, at Cambridge University, originated the device of keeping passwords in encrypted form rather than in clear, using for this purpose an encryption algorithm for which no reverse algorithm existed. It was discovered that many security loopholes were the result of optimizations introduced into the implementation. Such optimizations are essential if the system is to run at acceptable speed, but if they are not thought out with sufficient care, they are liable to breed security bugs. A notorious example is the delaying of the clearing of discarded blocks on the disk until new information comes to be written. It is quite possible to do this in a safe way, but there are hidden snags and many an implementor has fallen foul of them.

UNIX encrypts passwords, but does not take very good care of the file containing the encrypted form. As a result, penetrators have had some success in writing programs to break the encryption by a combination of guesswork and trial and error. Other systems do better than UNIX in safeguarding the encrypted passwords; it is likely that in future secure systems special attention will be given to the handling of password transactions and hiding the encrypted password files, perhaps by providing a dedicated secure server for this purpose.

As a result of this early history, security came to be seen as an aspect of the design of a time-sharing system. Beginning around 1980, efforts were set on foot to improve the security of leading proprietary time-sharing systems. These efforts, which were started well ahead of market demand, have achieved much success, largely by the patient identification and removal of implementation bugs, but also by the provision of better access control algorithms and audit trails. The security provided is now good enough for most business purposes, provided that the systems are used in a secure manner. Unfortunately, this cannot always be guaranteed. Users are apt to be careless about password discipline, and sometimes keep openly in their files copies of passwords that other users have entrusted to them. A further major source of insecurity is that many systems offer inherently insecure features, connected in particular with remote file transfer, that are an overhang from more trusting days. It is possible to disable these features, but system managers are reluctant to do so since users have grown accustomed to them, and find them useful.

With proprietary operating systems, each under the control of its respective vendor, there is every prospect that security once attained can be maintained. In particular, it is not in danger of being compromised by local modifications to the system. The coming of UNIX has changed all that. UNIX is vendor independent and exists in many variants, some of them official and some of them the result of local enterprise. Bringing all the versions and implementations up to a high security standard, and keeping them there, would be an impossible task. No doubt secure versions of UNIX will become available, but they will have to make their way in a fiercely competitive market in which security is only one consideration and it is unrealistic to expect that they will become dominant.

Confidence in the security of a system may be obtained by the regular kind of debugging and testing—to verify as far as possible that the implementation is a valid realization of the specification—and by inspection of the specification for security loopholes. It is sometimes suggested that it should be possible to give a formal proof that a system is secure. In principle, it is certainly possible to prove that a system meets its specification. However, insecurity results from its doing things that are not in the specification, for example, salting information away in hidden files. Proving that it does not do such things is equivalent to proving a negative, something that is proverbially difficult. Even if the technology of proving that programs meet their specifications were more advanced than it actually is, some major element of human inspection and certification would be necessary.

Much thought has been given to ways of making an inspector's task more straightforward, and anyone who has worked in the area is apt to have his own pet ideas. In one approach, the underlying idea is to reduce to a minimum the amount of code and data which is accessible to the running process at any given time. The inspector can then concentrate on that code and data and forget the rest. This involves making frequent changes in what is accessible and is, if everything is done in software, likely to lead to an intolerably low level of performance. Hardware aids have, therefore, been suggested.[11]

Much hope was later placed in the use of *capabilities*, or tickets, the mere possession of which gives the right to make use of some resource. The attraction of capabilities is that they do not imply any form of hierarchy as far as protection is concerned. Capabilities were discussed from the point of view of the writer of an operation system in Essay Eleven. As I there mentioned, experimental systems were demonstrated in which the capabilities were implemented in software, although it should have been clear from the beginning that such systems could not, for performance reasons, be of more than theoretical interest. When capabilities were implemented in hardware, it was found that their management led to great software complexity, a result which was as disappointing as it was unexpected. The final conclusion must be that, although the capability model makes it possible to show how some very desirable things could be done that are difficult to do any other way, it is of no use to us since efficient implementation is not possible.

It is perhaps as well that the search for hardware features that would support security was unfruitful, since they would inevitably have involved a loss of performance. Few people would have cared enough about security to accept this. Moreover, the industry was moving towards concentration on a small number of standard designs for processors, with a strong emphasis on performance. It is now clear that the solution to security problems must be found within that framework.

The Nature of Information

The military have a highly developed system for classifying documents and for giving a corresponding access classification to individuals. A corresponding degree of sophistication has not—so far, at any rate—been thought necessary in business. This difference of emphasis constitutes a major barrier between the two cultures.

One must be careful to distinguish between documents and information. The concept of information is an elusive one. In many ways information is like a gas which must be closely confined if it is not to escape. Outside a computer, information is bound by being written on paper; this implies that it is also bound to a form of words or symbols. A piece of paper is a physical object that can be handled and protected. Controls can be established so that only authorized people are allowed to see what is written on it and controls can be established over the copying of the information from one piece of paper to another.

If the information on the paper is read by a person, that information ceases to be bound either to the paper or to the form of words. It becomes part of what that person knows. It no longer exists as a distinct package nor is it subject to physical controls. In a similar way, if the contents of two bottles of gas are mixed, each parcel of gas loses its identity. If two different gases are to be kept in the same bottle, then there must be an impermeable membrane to separate them. The membrane must be non-porous and it must be free from pinholes. A single pinhole will suffice for the gases to become mixed. Naturally no one would store gases in this way unless he were absolutely certain that the membrane were impermeable.

When information is keyed into a time-shared computer and accessed by users in the course of their work, it is liable—if no precautions are taken—to become mixed up with other information in the computer. Computer operating systems make it possible for the owners of information to take such precautions by allowing them, at their discretion, to impose access controls on files. The question is whether controls established in this way can be made good enough to meet the highest security requirements. In other words, to pursue the gas metaphor, can the software controls within a time-shared computer be made sufficiently good to form a reliable, hole-free membrane?

Much research on operating systems has been directed to this problem. I do not question that a secure time-sharing system can be designed. I would even agree that it could be implemented in such a way that the probability of another user or a penetrator obtaining unauthorized access to a user's files would be negligibly small, even taking account of major system malfunction. However, I believe that such a system would necessarily be implemented on safety-first principles, and would run intolerably slowly. The optimizations necessary to make the system acceptable would carry with them many risks of introducing security loopholes, and a detailed certification of the implementation would be necessary. A major difficulty to date has been to develop effective methods of certifying that the barriers are really hole-free. However eminent the authority ultimately responsible for the certification, I would be extremely reluctant to entrust any sensitive information to such a time-sharing system. I am, however, aware that I am here expressing a personal view and that there are others who do not feel the same way.

However, I believe that the above problem is likely to lose its importance, since we may soon expect to have, instead of large single computers, groups of workstations and servers linked by a LAN and connected to the outside world through one or more gateways. In my view, the unit of security should then be the group as a whole. The responsibility for security against espionage or sabotage would rest with the designer of the software for the gateways, rather than with the designers of the operating systems for the individual workstations. I pursue this matter further in the next essay.

The use of computer programs to penetrate computer systems raises some interesting thoughts, not to say concern. It means that the slightest slip in the implementation of access controls can have the most serious consequences. The point is not a new one. Harry Hinsley, the official historian of British Intelligence in World War 2, remarked recently in my hearing that the enemy signals that Bletchley Park had such success in reading were encrypted by machines, and that machines were used for breaking the encryption. No comparable success in the routine reading of "old fashioned" manually operated book codes was ever achieved.

It is natural to ask whether computers could be programmed to verify that whoever is attempting to log in is a human being and not a computer. In other words, can a computer be programmed to determine whether it is in contact with a human being or with another computer. If it could, then a powerful defense against worms and such-like would be available. The question is a dual of the one on which Turing based the famous Turing test: can a human being determine whether he is communicating with a computer or with another human being?

References

Denning, Peter J., ed. *Computers Under Attack: Intruders, Worms, and Viruses.* Reading, Mass.: Addison-Wesley, 1990.

National Research Council. *Computers at Risk.* (Report of a System Security Study Committee chaired by David Clark.) Washington, D.C.: National Academy Press, 1991.

ESSAY EIGHTEEN

Computer Security in the Business World—Distributed Systems

Users of traditional time-sharing systems were drawn from a wide range of organizations and there was a need to prevent them from gaining unauthorized access to one another's files or, to put it more positively, to make sure that any sharing of files and resources was on a controlled basis. The assumption was made that each user was as suspicious of other users as he was of outsiders.

The coming of departmental time-sharing systems heralded a change of attitude. Such systems catered for a limited group of users who were in some way colleagues. There was no reason why they should take liberties with each other's resources, or pry into each other's private files, and indeed no serious harm was done if they did.

This points to a new attitude to security. It is better to think in terms of secure enclaves on the perimeter of which strict security is enforced. Within the enclave there is a lower degree of security or perhaps none at all. Departmental time-sharing systems are now giving way to groups of workstations and file servers tied together by an ethernet. The enclave model of security is highly appropriate to such systems.

If the enclave is formed of a single minicomputer, or a workstation used as such, its operating system is responsible for preventing unauthorized access by people outside, whether they make their approach via a network or by attempting to dial in. Groups of workstations or personal computers on an ethernet are best connected to the outside world via separate computers dedicated to the purpose, and connected both to the ethernet and to external links. Such computers are known as *gateways*. Security is enforced by the software running in the gateways.

Making an Enclave Secure

The first step in establishing a secure enclave is to control remote log-in. Ideally, this should not be allowed at all. A distant user wishing to be connected to a computer inside the enclave, whether via a computer network or via the public telephone system, should make a request through some external channel; for example, he might make a telephone call or send a request via an insecure computer on the net. If his request is agreed to, then the connection is set up by a person working from inside the secure enclave. More commonly, but less securely, the distant user is allowed to log in briefly in order to register a request that he should be called back. The merit of the call-back procedure is that it establishes the location from which the distant user is working. Call-back will become less necessary as telephone systems which automatically provide this information come into use.

The problem is essentially one of user authentication. In order to give a high degree of protection, authentication must go beyond simply requiring the applicant to quote a password or use an encryption key. Ideally there should be identification of the individual as such; that is, it should be ascertained beyond reasonable doubt that the applicant is the person he or she claims to be. There are various ways in which this can be done. For example, applicants can be required to speak on the telephone to a colleague who knows them well and who can vouch for them. Another method is by use of a *challenge-response box*, containing an encryption algorithm and a key that has been set by the system manager. The computer sends the applicant a random number. He or she encrypts this number using the box and sends the result back to the computer, where it is compared with a locally encrypted version. Business users are already beginning to take advantage of these and other advances made in authentication techniques. Authentications should have a finite and fairly short life, at the end of which users should be required to re-authenticate themselves.

There are many reasons why it is not a sufficient form of authentication for the distant computer to require the simple quotation of a password. In the first place, passwords can be stolen or guessed; worse than that, experience shows that, where such systems are in operation, users invariably keep passwords to other computers in their files, so that if those files are penetrated the other computers also become accessible to the penetrator.

Some operating systems allow distant callers to deposit information into a user's files, bypassing the password system altogether. They may even allow programs to be deposited and activated. Such facilities are obviously dangerous. It is particularly unfortunate that they were at one time used to implement mail systems. Since such mail systems can, in certain circumstances, be used to deliver and activate Trojan horses,[12] a tendency grew up for all computer mail systems to be viewed with exaggerated suspicion.

Safe equivalents for nearly all the services that have in the past been implemented in an unsafe way can be provided. If some of them are not quite as convenient as the unsafe ones, then this is a price that must be paid for security. However, I do not myself think that the unsafe methods will be greatly missed, except in certain computer science circles. Any form of information transfer between computers has its hazards, especially if it is used for the distribution of software. There are many ways in which a user may be tricked into accepting and running a piece of software which contains a Trojan horse. In the last resort, one must depend on the integrity and alertness of the users.

The way in which businesses are organized lends itself naturally to the establishment of secure enclaves. For example, the financial department is likely to have information that is sensitive in the stock exchange sense—what is known as insider information. This can conveniently be kept in a special computer, which can only be accessed from terminals securely located in the financial department itself and connected to the computer in a secure manner. Those who access it actually work in the financial department and are, by the nature of their duties, entitled to have access. If the financial department computer has no hardware facilities for outsiders to log in through a network (but only facilities for users on that computer to send information to other computers) it can be very secure. People outside the financial department will have to request information to be sent to them over direct links. Such links between computers are to be compared to doors that can only be opened from the inside. Outsiders must knock on the door for attention and their credentials are checked before their requests are approved.

Management-Oriented Security

It has been said that war is too serious a matter to be left to the generals. I believe that computer security is too serious a matter to be left to computer experts. Managers at all levels in an organization should be able to understand how information flows from one departmental computer system to another and be able to take action to stop or restrict the flow across critical boundaries if they perceive their business to have come under threat. This would have been an impossible challenge in the days of large central computer systems. It is the coming of departmental systems that has made it possible to contemplate.

Conceptually, the most secure computer configuration for a business would consist of a set of departmental systems with no wires passing between them. When necessary, information would be transferred from one system to another by writing a magnetic disk and carrying it across. Given such a system, any manager can understand what is going on. Since some identifiable person is responsible for writing the disk and transferring it, the manager can control the flow of information in the same way as he controls other things.

If a gateway and telephone line are used for transfer, efficiency will be improved. The manager will still be able to understand how the system works, but he will need to be able to assure himself that transmission is possible in one direction only. To make him fully happy, there should be a conspicuous switch that will allow the modem to be disconnected from the line. If he is worried enough, the manager can stand by the switch and only let through information if he sees fit!

Security depends on the integrity of the software in the gateway and it is desirable that this should be loaded through an input device directly connected to the gateway itself. This has the merit of simplicity and can be understood, along with the security hazards that attend it, by the manager. In a highly stable environment, the software could be burned into read-only memory.

Other facilities can be added. Each will bring new risks. I believe that it is possible to add all essential facilities in such a way that a non-technical manager can still understand how the system works and be able to intervene in an emergency. Any facility that cannot be so added should be done without.

If remote log-in is required, the remarks I made above—about the need for rigorous authentication of the user, and the need for the connection to be set up from within the enclave concerned—all apply. The guiding principle is that a user who is allowed remote log-in should be allowed to log in to his own enclave and no other. When logged in, he will then be in the same position as he would be in if he were in his own office. No one who is not to be regarded as a full member of an enclave should be allowed to log in at all. A manager should have no difficulty in understanding how this system is intended to work, although he will need to depend, more than he may wish, on assurances from his expert advisors that there are no loopholes.

Shared Information Systems

Central shared databases and other information systems have an important role to play in business organizations. This role is supplementary to that played by departmental computers. When information has been cleared for general or selective release, it can be transferred to a central database. For example, one of the duties of staff in the financial department might be to pass, from time to time, selected information to a database where it will be available for access by those throughout the company who need it.

Fortunately, provided that a sufficiently secure procedure for authenticating users can be put in place, making a shared database secure is relatively straightforward compared with making a general-purpose time-sharing system secure. This is because users cannot run arbitrary programs on databases in the way they can on a time-sharing system. All they can do is to invoke one of a small set of services provided.

It remains true that there are serious security risks in running any central information system. However, these do not arise primarily because of possible loopholes in the software. They arise because of the danger of human error in selecting the information to be stored and in setting the access controls.

References

Denning, Peter J., ed. *Computers Under Attack: Intruders, Worms, and Viruses*. Reading, Mass.: Addison-Wesley, 1990.

National Research Council. *Computers at Risk*. (Report of a System Security Study Committee chaired by David Clark.) Washington, D.C.: National Academy Press, 1991.

Endnotes

1. (page 9) In the original version of this essay (*CACM,* vol. 35, no.3 [March 1992], p. 15), I remarked that the details of how Babbage intended programs to be written at the user level were far from clear. However, very recent research, undertaken by Allan Bromley among Babbage's voluminous writings and drawings of the 1840s, has brought to light several draft lists of the operations that an operation card might direct the engine to perform. These correspond to the instruction set of a modern computer, although the correspondence is not an exact one because Babbage had separate cards for operations and variables. I am grateful to Dr. Bromley for allowing me to refer to his research.

2. (page 10) I have endeavored to give my impression of Babbage's personality in a one-act play entitled "Pray Mr. Babbage . . . A Character Study in Dramatic Form." (See Wilkes, 1991 in Essay One "References.")

3. (page 11) This information comes from an unpublished letter from Herschel Babbage, then living in St. Mary's Adelaide, South Australia, postmarked 13 May 1853. I am indebted to Mr. Garry Tee for allowing me to see a photograph that he took of this letter, with the permission of the owner.

4. (page 15) It was a great step forward in the days of desk machine computation to be able to compute a difference table rapidly and accurately. It made differences of practical as well as of theoretical importance. It is abundantly clear that the use of high-order differences as a means of detecting errors in tables had not occurred to Babbage. He designed his Difference Engine for sub-tabulation only, and it would not have been possible to use it to compute differences.

5. (page 35) A fully researched history of personal computers has still to be written. I have drawn heavily on Williams and Welch, 1985 and on Garetz, 1985. (See Essay Four "References.")

6. (page 39) It is something of an irony that microprogramming reached microprocessors just at the time when the RISC movement was making it unnecessary.

7. (page 55) Both the MIPS R4000 and the Intel i860 took longer to reach the market than optimistic forecasts suggested they would. The R4000 became a popular processor for use in workstations. However, the i860 did not appeal to workstation designers. The reason for this appears to be that the interface to the software did not well support process changing and efficient handling of interrupts. However, the i860 was used in other applications, notably in a highly parallel computer designed by Intel.

8. (page 77) Snoopy caches are so called because each cache listens to the traffic passing on the bus and takes action when necessary; for example, it may update or invalidate its own entry relating to a certain word when it hears a more recent value being written to main memory from elsewhere. The first paper to appear on the subject was by J. Goodman in 1983, but the idea had apparently occurred independently to several people at about the same time. (See Goodman, 1983 in Essay Eight "References.")

9. (page 123) The difficulty can be concisely stated by saying that a digital computer is a finite automaton and as such cannot simulate in a general manner a system with an infinite number of degrees of freedom. This point is worth stressing, since there is a widespread impression that all that is necessary is to make the number of degrees of freedom large. For example, in the case of the ordinary differential equation discussed in the text, it is suggested that the range of the independent variable need only be divided into a sufficiently large number of intervals. It is true that, if this is done, the number of independent solutions of the differential equation which are close approximations to solutions of the differential equation can be increased indefinitely, but there will always be other solutions—the more highly oscillatory ones—which bear no such relationship. These solutions are nothing more nor less than artifacts, and they arise directly from the discretization of the continuous variable.

Very often, it is possible to proceed in such a way that the artifacts have no deleterious effect and in this case the computer may be made to simulate the continuous system to a high degree of accuracy. In other cases, however, it is not possible. Anyone who doubts the truth of this statement should read the literature on the numerical solution of what are known as *stiff* differential equations. These equations exhibit the problem in an extreme form, and no entirely satisfactory general method has been found for dealing with them. The straightforward approach of working with a very small interval in the argument can lead to solution times measured in years.

10. (page 149) L.G. Roberts of ARPA was clearly aware of this possibility, because in a paper presented to the First Symposium on Operating System Principles held in October 1967, he said:

> In addition to computer network activities, a network can be used to handle interpersonal message transmissions. This type of service can also be used for educational courses and conference activities. However, it is not an important motivation for a network of scientific computers.

11. (page 170) The hardware features here discussed provide memory protection; that is, they make it possible to place specified parts of the memory out of bounds to the running process. Apart from its value in connection with computer security, memory protection is necessary to prevent users' programs accidentally corrupting code belonging to the operating system. The term "system integrity" is sometimes used with reference to this requirement.

12. (page 177) In the second book of the Aeneid, Virgil describes how the Greeks, having failed to reduce Troy by siege, resolved to try a strategem. They built a large wooden horse, placed it temptingly outside the city walls, and then sailed away apparently for good. The Trojans foolishly dragged the wooden horse into the city, not suspecting that, concealed

in its belly, were armed men. At dead of night, when the garrison were sleeping off the effects of their victory celebrations, the armed men emerged and let in the main Greek army which had by then come back. The metaphor of the Trojan horse is aptly used to describe a piece of software which an unsuspecting user accepts as a gift and finds too late that it has damaged his system.

General References

Encyclopedia

Ralston, Anthony and Edwin D. Reilly, eds. *Encyclopedia of Computer Science,* 3rd ed. New York: Van Nostrand Reinhold, 1993. [Highly recommended as a source of concise and reliable information. Contains articles on early computers, software history, parallel processing, architectures, etc.]

History

1. Proc. Symp. on Large Scale Digital Calculating Machinery, 7–10 January 1947. In *Annals of the Computation Laboratory of Harvard University,* vol XVI. Cambridge: Harvard University Press, 1948.
2. Wilkes, M.V., ed. Report on a Conference on High Speed Automatic Computing Machines, July 22–25, 1949. University Mathematical Laboratory, Cambridge, England. Reprinted in *The Early British Computer Conferences,* vol. 14, eds. M.R. Williams and M. Campbell-Kelly. *Charles Babbage Institute Reprint Series for the History of Computing*. Cambridge: MIT Press, 1989.
3. Goldstine, Herman H. *The Computer From Pascal to von Neumann*. Princeton, N.J.: Princeton University Press, 1972.
4. Metropolis, N., J. Howlett, and Gian-Carlo Rota. *A History of Computing in the Twentieth Century*. New York: Academic Press, 1980. [Papers presented at an international conference held in Los Alamos, New Mexico, June 1976.]
5. Randell, Brian, ed. *Origins of Digital Computers: Selected Papers,* 3rd ed. Berlin: Springer-Verlag, 1982.
6. Augarten, Stan. *Bit by Bit: An Illustrated History of Computers*. New York: Ticknor and Fields, 1984.

7. *Annals of the History of Computing* [A periodical devoted to the history of computing, now published by the IEEE. The first issue appeared in 1979.]

Programming Languages

1. Wexelblat, Richard L., ed. *History of Programming Languages.* New York: Academic Press, 1981. [A report of the ACM SIGPLAN conference on the history of programming languages held in January 1978.]
2. Proc. 2nd ACM SIGPLAN History of Programming Languages Conference, April, 1993. *ACM SIGPLAN Notices,* vol. 28, no. 3 (1993).

Index

G

H

P

Q

R

X

Z

About the Author

Maurice V. Wilkes was born in England in 1913. He went up to Cambridge University in 1931 and studied mathematical physics and other subjects. In 1934 he became a research student in the Cavendish Laboratory where he did experimental work on the propagation of radio waves in the ionosphere. This led to an interest in tidal motion in the earth's atmosphere, and his first book was on this subject. It also led to an interest in computing methods and he was appointed in 1937 to a junior faculty position with a view to his assisting with the planning of a Computing Laboratory, or Mathematical Laboratory as it was eventually called. When Wilkes returned to Cambridge in 1945 after war service, he became head of the Mathematical Laboratory, which many years later was renamed the Computer Laboratory.

In the summer of 1946, Wilkes attended the famous course of lectures on electronic computers held at the Moore School in Philadelphia. On his return, he set about building up a well qualified team and started work on the design and construction of the computer known as the EDSAC. The EDSAC first began to work in June 1949, and the team turned its attention to programming methodology. This work led to the publication in 1951, by Wilkes and two colleagues, of the first book to appear on computer programming.

Support for the computer industry has always been high on the list of Wilkes's priorities, and he and his laboratory made some important contributions. They helped Leo Computers to design a successful computer which was based closely on the EDSAC and was intended for office applications. Wilkes's ideas for microprogramming, presented at a conference at Manchester University in 1951, were widely taken up by the computer industry some ten years later, when the development of semi-conductor devices was sufficiently advanced. A note by Wilkes published in 1965 drew attention to the possibilities latent in slave memories, later known as cache memories. This was the first paper to be published on cache memories.

Wilkes was active in the early days of time-sharing, and in 1967 he published a book based largely on his experience with the CTSS at MIT and with the Cambridge Multiple Access System developed in his own laboratory.

Time-sharing directed the attention of the computer research community to computer security and the need for improved systems of memory protection. Wilkes initiated a project designed to investigate the use of hardware capabilities. There was widespread interest in this subject in the 1970s, although the idea has not stood the test of time. In connection with the project, an experimental computer was designed and built in the Computer Laboratory, and an account of it was given in 1979 in a book written by Wilkes in collaboration with R.M. Needham.

In 1974, it appeared to Wilkes that semi-conductor development had reached the point at which wide-band local area networks, based on computer technology rather than on traditional telecommunication technology, were feasible. The design study for what became known as the Cambridge Ring was first published in 1975. This led to the development of the Cambridge Model Distributed System, based on the Cambridge Ring and described by Wilkes and Needham in 1980.

In 1980, Wilkes retired from his position as head of the Computer Laboratory and went to work for the Digital Equipment Corporation at their central engineering headquarters in Maynard, Massachusetts. While there he became chairman of a committee dealing with research and advanced development. When he left in 1986 he was serving as Associate Director, on behalf of DEC, of Project Athena at MIT. For several years he was also an Adjunct Professor in the Department of Electrical Engineering and Computer Science at MIT. In 1985, he published a volume of Memoirs.

On his return to England in 1986, Wilkes became Member for Research Strategy on the Olivetti Research Board. He is currently adviser to Olivetti research strategy.

About the Author

Wilkes was for many years head of the Computer Laboratory of the University of Cambridge. Since 1980 he has worked in industry, first with DEC in Massachusetts and now with Olivetti Research in Cambridge, England. He is a Distinguished Fellow of the British Computer Society, and he was recently named as one of the first Fellows of the ACM. He is a Fellow of the Royal Society, and a Fellow of the Royal Academy of Engineering. He is a Foreign Associate of both the U.S. National Academy of Sciences and the U.S. National Academy of Engineering. He was the recipient of the 1992 Kyoto Prize for Advanced Technology.

In 1967, Wilkes delivered the Turing Lecture and in 1980 he received the Eckert-Mauchly award. In 1985, he published *Memoirs of a Computer Pioneer* (MIT Press). He was a member of the ACM Council from 1991 to 1994.